MODERN
HOME
ATLAS

MODERN HOME ATLAS

GEORGE PHILIP

Edited by
B.M.WILLETT

CONTENTS

British Library Cataloguing in Publication Data

Modern home atlas – 7th ed.
1. Atlases, British
912   G1021

ISBN 0-540-05525-5

Illustrations

Half-title: evening light on Thamserku, Nepal (*Bruce Coleman*).
Title: Bryce Canyon, Utah, USA (*Bruce Coleman*). **Contents:** Tahiti
with the island of Moorea in the distance (*Bruce Coleman*).
Front cover: the Great Pyramids of Giza, and Kingfisher
(*Bruce Coleman*)

GENERAL REFERENCE

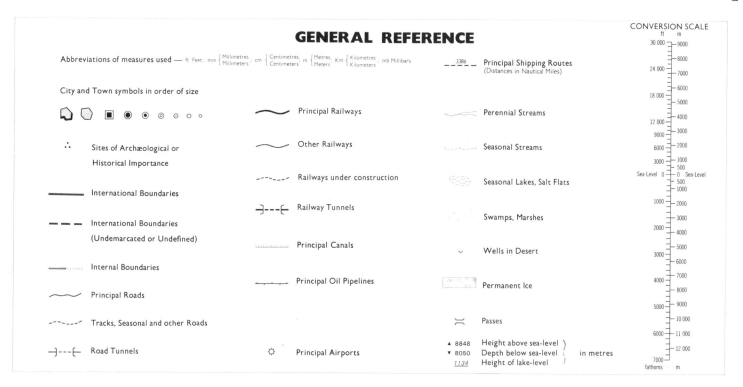

Abbreviations of measures used — ft Feet; mm {Millimetres / Millimeters} cm {Centimetres / Centimeters} m {Metres / Meters} Km {Kilometres / Kilometers} mb Millibars

City and Town symbols in order of size

∴ Sites of Archæological or Historical Importance

International Boundaries

International Boundaries (Undemarcated or Undefined)

Internal Boundaries

Principal Roads

Tracks, Seasonal and other Roads

Road Tunnels

Principal Railways

Other Railways

Railways under construction

Railway Tunnels

Principal Canals

Principal Oil Pipelines

☼ Principal Airports

Principal Shipping Routes (Distances in Nautical Miles)

Perennial Streams

Seasonal Streams

Seasonal Lakes, Salt Flats

Swamps, Marshes

Wells in Desert

Permanent Ice

Passes

▲ 8848 Height above sea-level
▼ 8050 Depth below sea-level   in metres
1134 Height of lake-level

CONVERSION SCALE

THE WORLD
Physical
1:150 000 000

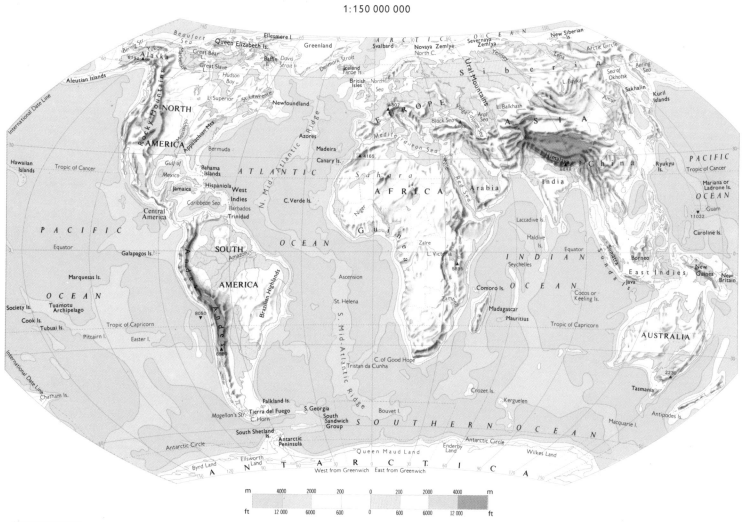

m 4000 2000 200 0 200 2000 4000 m
ft 12 000 6000 600 0 600 6000 12 000 ft

Projection: Hammer Equal Area

COPYRIGHT: GEORGE PHILIP & SON. LTD.

Projection : Hammer Equal Area

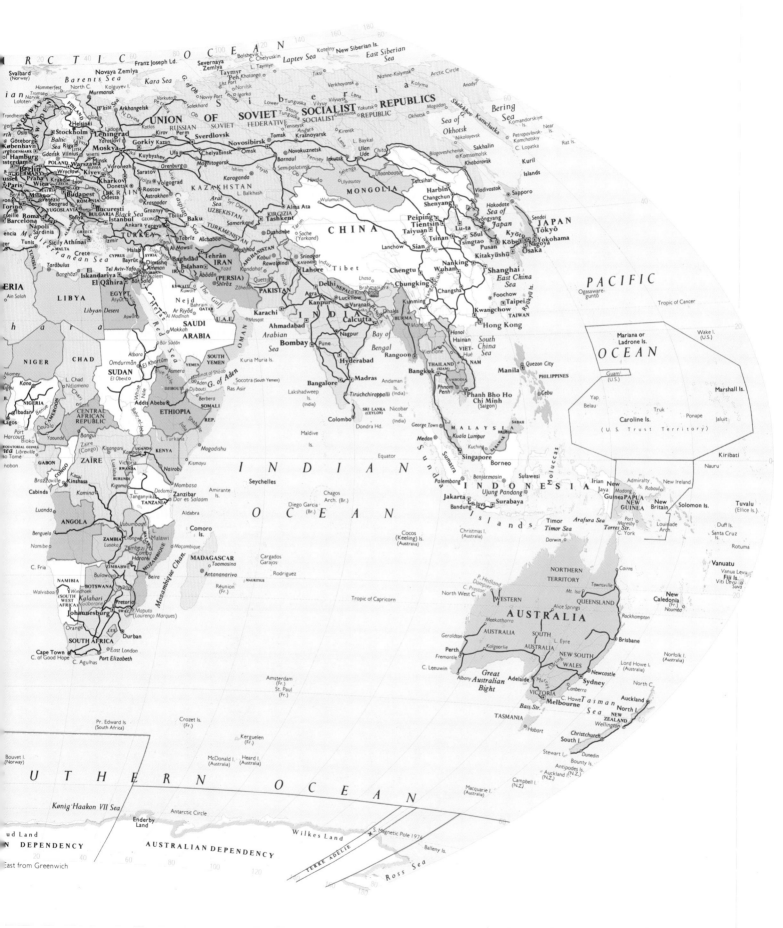

1:20 000 000

100 0 100 200 300 400 500 miles
100 0 200 400 600 800 km

ATLANTIC OCEAN

NORWEGIAN SEA

NORTH SEA

BALTIC SEA

BLACK SEA

CASPIAN SEA

ADRIATIC SEA

MEDITERRANEAN SEA

Tyrrhenian Sea

Ligurian Sea

Ionian Sea

Aegean Sea

Sea of Marmara

White Sea

Sea of Azov

Iceland

British Isles

Great Britain

Ireland

Iberian Peninsula

Scandinavia

Finland

Lapland

Tundra

Ural Mountains

Obshchiy Syrt

Volga Uplands

Central Russian Uplands

Russian Plain

Ukraine

Pripyat Marshes

North European Plain

Carpathians

Alps

Pyrenees

Apennines

Dinaric Alps

Balkans

Balkan Peninsula

Caucasus

Anatolia

Kurdistan

Armenia

Plain of Hungary

Wallachia

Transylvanian Alps

Morea

Crete

Cyprus

Sicily

Sardinia

Corsica

Malta

Kola Peninsula

Kanin Peninsula

Gulf of Bothnia

Gulf of Finland

Gulf of Riga

Gotland

North Cape

Nordkinn

Bay of Biscay

English Channel

Cantabrian Mts.

Sierra Morena

Sierra Nevada

Andalusia

Old Castile

New Castile

Central Massif

Ardennes

Vosges

Harz

Black For.

Plateau of the Shotts

Maritime Atlas

Str. of Gibraltar

Str. of Otranto

Str. of Messina

Str. of Bonifacio

Gulf of Lions

Faeroes

Shetland Is.

Orkney Is.

Hebrides

Brittany

ft m
12 000 4000
6000 2000
3000 1000
1200 400
600 200
0 0
600 200
2000 6000
4000 12 000
m ft

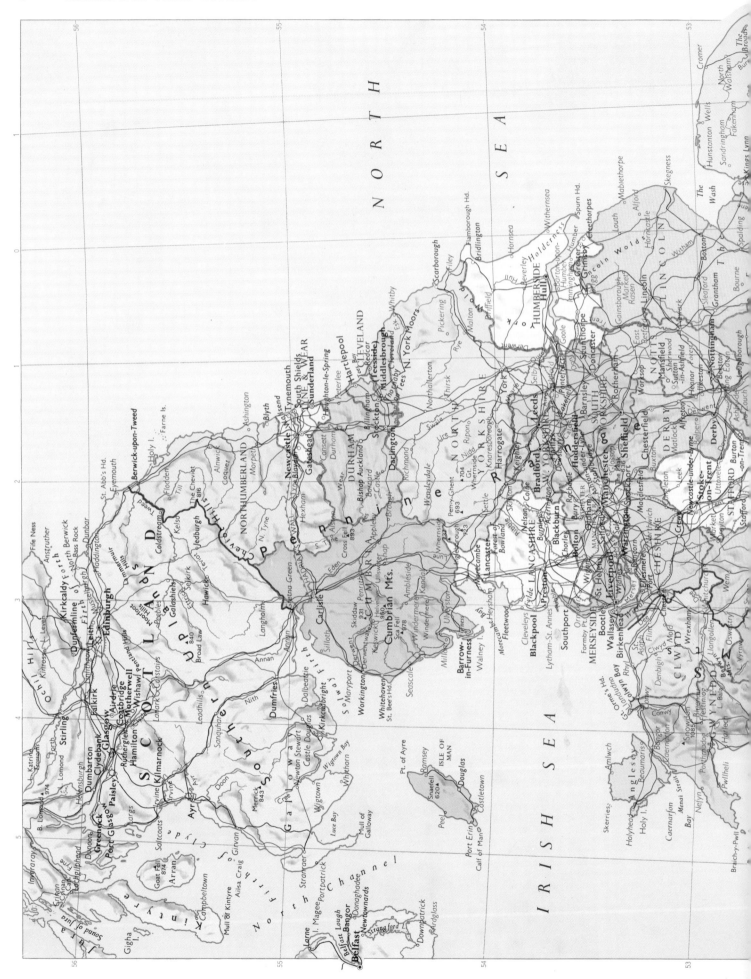

1:2 000 000

10   0   10   20   30   40   50 miles
10   0   10 20 30 40 50 60 70 80 km

East from Greenwich

West from Greenwich

Projection - Conical with two standard parallels.

E N G L I S H   C H A N N E L

F R A N C E

Rouen
Dieppe
Le Tréport
St-Valery-en-Caux
Fécamp
Étretat
C. d' Antifer
C. de la Hève
Le Havre
Honfleur
Trouville
Deauville
Pont l' Évêque
Lisieux
Bernay
Louviers
Elbeuf
Yvetot
Caudebec
Seine
Yerville
Arromanches
Vierville
Bayeux
Caen
Isigny
Carentan
Périers
St-Lô
Barfleur
Quineville
Valognes
Cherbourg
C. de la Hague
Alderney
Guernsey
St. Peter Port
Sark
Jersey
St. Helier
Channel Islands
Barneville
Coutances

SCILLY ISLES
On same scale
St. Ives
Penzance
Land's End
Isles of Scilly
St. Mary's

SUFFOLK
Lowestoft
Beccles
Southwold
Bungay
Saxmundham
Aldeburgh
Orford
Orford Ness
Sizewell
Diss
Stowmarket
Woodbridge
Felixstowe
Harwich
The Naze
Walton-on-the-Naze
Ipswich
Sudbury
Needham
Mildenhall
Brandon
Thetford
Breckland
Bury St. Edmunds
Newmarket
Cambridge
St. Ives
Huntingdon
Flitton
Peterborough
Kettering
Corby
Market Harborough
Wellingborough
Rushden

CAMBRIDGE
ESSEX
Colchester
Clacton
Mersea
Maldon
Braintree
Halstead
Haverhill
Saffron Walden
Royston
Chelmsford
Brentwood
Basildon
Southend
Shoeburyness
Canvey I.
Rochford

HERTFORD
BEDFORD
Bedford
Biggleswade
Hitchin
Letchworth
Stevenage
Luton
Dunstable
Hemel Hempstead
Watford
St. Albans
Hertford
Ware
Bishops Stortford
Harlow
Epping
Enfield
Barnet
Harrow
Hillingdon
Uxbridge
Slough
Windsor
Maidenhead
High Wycombe
Beaconsfield

LONDON
Romford
Havering
Barking
Redbridge
Brent
Richmond
Croydon
Bromley
Dartford
Gravesend
Greenwich
Woolwich

KENT
Rochester
Chatham
Gillingham
Sittingbourne
Sheerness
Isle of Sheppey
Whitstable
Herne Bay
Margate
Ramsgate
North Foreland
Broadstairs
Canterbury
Sandwich
Deal
Dover
South Foreland
Folkestone
Hythe
New Romney
Romney Marsh
Dungeness
Ashford
Maidstone
Tonbridge
Tunbridge Wells
Sevenoaks
Edenbridge
Rye
Thanet
Medway

NORTHAMPTON
Northampton
Daventry
Rugby
Nuneaton
Hinckley
Leamington
Warwick
Stratford-on-Avon
Redditch

WEST MIDLANDS
Birmingham
Coventry
Solihull
Sutton Coldfield
West Bromwich
Dudley
Tipton
Stourbridge
Brierley Hill
Wolverhampton

WARWICK

SHROPSHIRE
Bridgnorth
Ludlow
Clee Hills
Kidderminster
Leominster
Bromyard

HEREFORD & WORCESTER
Worcester
Hereford
Malvern
Malvern Hills
Ledbury
Ross-on-Wye
Evesham
Cheltenham
Tewkesbury
Cleeve Hills 330

GLOUCESTER
Gloucester
Stroud
Cirencester
Cheltenham
Forest of Dean
Monmouth

OXFORD
Oxford
Banbury
Bicester
Witney
Woodstock
Abingdon
Wantage
Faringdon

BUCKS
Buckingham
Milton Keynes
Aylesbury
Thame

BERKS
Reading
Newbury
Maidenhead
Wokingham
Bracknell
White Horse Hill
Berkshire Downs
Lambourn
Kennet

WILTS
Swindon
Marlborough
Devizes
Chippenham
Calne
Trowbridge
Melksham
Warminster
Salisbury
Salisbury Plain
Stonehenge
Amesbury
Mere
Wilton

AVON
Bristol
Bath
Weston-super-Mare
Clevedon
Avonmouth
Keynsham

SOMERSET
Taunton
Bridgwater
Yeovil
Wells
Glastonbury
Frome
Shepton Mallet
Bruton
Wellington
Minehead
Chard
Crewkerne
Wincanton
Mendip Hills
Quantock Hills
Polden Hills
Somerton
Ilminster
Langport
Parrett
Brue

DORSET
Dorchester
Weymouth
Portland Bill
Bridport
Blandford
Sherborne
Shaftesbury
Poole
Bournemouth
Swanage
I. of Purbeck
St. Alban's Hd.
Wareham
Stour
Lyme Regis
Beaminster
Portland I.

HANTS
Winchester
Southampton
Eastleigh
Romsey
Andover
Basingstoke
Fleet
Aldershot
Farnborough
Alton
Petersfield
Portsmouth
Gosport
Fareham
Havant
Fawley
Lymington
Ringwood
New Forest
Test
Itchen
Christchurch

ISLE OF WIGHT
Newport
Cowes
Ryde
Sandown
Ventnor
Needles
St. Catherine's Point
Selsey Bill
Hayling I.

SURREY
Guildford
Woking
Farnham
Haslemere
Godalming
Dorking
Reigate
Redhill
Leatherhead
Epsom
Esher
Leith Hill 294
Caterham

WEST SUSSEX
Chichester
Bognor Regis
Littlehampton
Worthing
Crawley
Horsham
Haywards Heath
Midhurst
Petworth
Arundel
The Downs

EAST SUSSEX
Brighton
Hove
Lewes
Newhaven
Seaford
Beachy Hd.
Eastbourne
Bexhill
Hastings
Battle
Uckfield
East Grinstead
Crowborough
Ashdown Forest

The Weald

DEVON
Exeter
Exmouth
Sidmouth
Honiton
Teignmouth
Dawlish
Tiverton
Torquay (Torbay)
Paignton
Dartmouth
Newton Abbot
Totnes
Kingsbridge
Salcombe
Start Pt.
Plymouth
Devonport
Tavistock
Okehampton
Crediton
Barnstaple
Bideford
Braunton
Ilfracombe
Lynton
Holsworthy
South Molton
Dartmoor
Exmoor
Dunkery Beacon 520
Yes Tor 618
Taw
Torridge
Teign
Exe
Bovey Tracey

CORNWALL
Launceston
Bude
Bodmin
Bodmin Moor
Brown Willy 419
Liskeard
Looe
Fowey
St. Austell
Truro
Newquay
Padstow
Boscastle
Wadebridge
Camborne
Redruth
Helston
St. Ives
Penzance
St. Michael's Mount
Lizard
Falmouth
Eddystone

WALES
Cardigan Bay
Aberdovey
Aberystwyth
Aberaeron
New Quay
Cardigan
Fishguard
St. David's Hd.
St. David's
St. Bride's Bay
Haverfordwest
Milford Haven
Pembroke
Tenby
Carmarthen
Llanelli
Kidwelly
Burry Port
Llandovery
Llandeilo
Ammanford
Llangadog
Lampeter
Newcastle Emlyn
Tregaron

DYFED
POWYS
Newtown
Montgomery
Welshpool
Llanidloes
Rhayader
Builth Wells
Llandrindod Wells
Knighton
Presteigne
Radnor Forest
Llanfair
Black Mts.

GWENT
Newport
Abergavenny
Pontypool
Cwmbran
Chepstow
Monmouth
Usk

MID GLAMORGAN
WEST GLAMORGAN
SOUTH GLAMORGAN
Cardiff
Swansea
Neath
Port Talbot
Bridgend
Barry
Penarth
Merthyr Tydfil
Aberdare
Rhondda
Pontypridd
Maesteg
Mountain Ash
Caerphilly
Gower
Porthcawl
Brecon
Brecon Beacons 886

Bristol Channel
Lundy
Hartland Point

Severn
Wye
Taff
Tawe
Towy

1 : 2 000 000

10 0 10 20 30 40 50 miles
10 0 10 20 30 40 50 60 70 80 km

ORKNEY IS.
On same scale

Orkney Is.
Hoy Scapa Flow South Ronaldsay
North Ronaldsay
Westray
Rousay Eday Sanday
Stromness Mainland Shapinsay Stronsay
Hoy Kirkwall ORKNEY
Scapa Flow
South Ronaldsay
Pentland Firth
Dunnet Hd.
John O'Groats

Pentland Firth
Dunnet Hd.
Strathy Pt.
C. Wrath
Durness Tongue Halladale Thurso Dounreay
Ben Hope 927 Naver Wick
Reay Forest Noss Hd.
L. Laxford Lybster
Eddrachillis Bay Helmsdale Ord of Caithness
Lochinver Enard Bay L. Assynt B. More Assynt Loch Shin Brora Helmsdale
Ullapool L. Shin Lairg Brora
L. Broom Oykell Golspie
B. Dearg 1081 Dornoch
WESTERN Dornoch Firth
Tarbat Ness
ISLES L. Fannich Tain Moray Firth
Gairloch Ben Wyvis 1045 Cromarty Lossiemouth Cullen Portsoy Banff Macduff Kinnaird's Head
Strathpeffer Elgin Buckie BUCHAN Fraserburgh
Flannan Is. L. Roag Broad Bay Conon Nairn Forres Rothes Keith Rattray Head
Stornoway Torridon Dingwall Fortrose Deveron Turriff Peterhead
Lewis Eye Pen. Beauly GRAMPIAN Huntly Buchan Ness
Harris INVERNESS Grantown-on-Spey Dufftown Ellon Ythan
Tarbert Beauly Culloden Moor Findhorn Inverurie
North Uist Lochmaddy L. Seaforth Farrar HIGHLAND Aviemore Tomintoul Alford Don
Monadhliath Mts. Strath Spey ABERDEEN
Benbecula Glen Affric Kingussie Cairn Gorm Mts. Aboyne Girdle Ness
Monach Is. Glen Moriston Fort Augustus Newtonmore Cairn Toul 1292 Macdhui 1311 Ballater Banchory
South Uist Skye Dornie Lochalsh L. Oich Cairngorm Braemar Balmoral Stonehaven
Lochboisdale Kyle Glen Garry Badenoch Lochnagar 1154 Braes of Angus Laurencekirk
Ben More Raasay Glen Spean Forest of Atholl Inverbervie
Canna Cuillin Hills Loch Arkaig Garry Blair Atholl N. Esk Brechin
Barra Rhum Cuillin Sound Mallaig L. Morar Grampian Highlands Pass of Killiecrankie Kirriemuir S. Esk Montrose
Eigg Arisaig L. Arkaig Pitlochry Forfar
Barra Hd. Muck L. Moidart Fort William Ben 1343 Nevis Aberfeldy Tummel Alyth Arbroath
Pt. of Ardnamurchan L. Shiel L. Eil Rannoch Moor L. Rannoch Tay Blairgowrie
Coll Ardgour Glen Moor Ballachulish Ben Lawers 1214 L. Tay Dunkeld Sidlaw Hills
Morvern Lismore Breadalbane Killin Tay TAYSIDE S Dundee Broughty Ferry
Tobermory Sound of Mull Ben Cruachan 1124 Scone Firth of Tay NORTH
Tiree Mull Ben More 966 Oban Ben More 1174 Perth Tayport SEA
Staffa Iona Firth of Lorn Loch Awe B. Vorlich 942 Crieff St. Andrews
Inveraray B. Vorlich 983 Callander Earn FIFE Fife Ness
ATLANTIC Ben Lomond 974 L. Katrine Trossachs Kinross Leven Anstruther
OCEAN Colonsay L. Lomond CENTRAL Dunblane Cowdenbeath Buckhaven
Stirling Alloa Glenrothes Kirkcaldy Bass Rock
Crinan Bannockburn Dunfermline North Berwick
Rubh a' Mhail Jura Helensburgh Grangemouth Rosyth Firth of Forth Dunbar
Islay Sound of Jura Dunoon Dumbarton Falkirk Linlithgow Leith St. Abbs Hd.
Bowmore Gigha Clydebank Cumbernauld Edinburgh LOTHIAN Haddington Eyemouth
Port Ellen Kintyre STRATHCLYDE Greenock GLASGOW Airdrie Livingston Musselburgh Holy I.
Renfrew Coatbridge Bathgate Dalkeith Berwick-upon-Tweed
Paisley Motherwell Pentland Hills Peebles Duns
Johnstone Rutherglen Wishaw Moorfoot Hills Lammermuir Hills
E. Kilbride Hamilton Carstairs Coldstream Flodden Till
Ardrossan Saltcoats Lanark Biggar Tweed Galashiels Kelso
Goat Fell 874 Irvine Kilmarnock BORDERS Melrose The Cheviot 816
Arran Brodick Troon Prestwick Ayr Broad Law 840 Selkirk Jedburgh
Campbeltown Ayr Cumnock Ettrick Hawick Cheviot Hills
Ailsa Craig Girvan Leadhills Teviot Coquet
Rathlin Fair Hd. SOUTH Sanquhar Moffat N. Tyne
Ballycastle Mull of Kintyre Merrick 843 Nith Langholm ENGLAND
L. Ryan DUMFRIES Lockerbie Hexham
NORTHERN Stranraer AND Dumfries Gretna Green Esk HADRIAN'S WALL
Ballymena Larne Newton Stewart Castle Douglas GALLOWAY Annan Carlisle S. Tyne
IRELAND Portpatrick Wigtown Dalbeattie Solway Firth Alston
Ballybofey Whithorn Kirkcudbright Derwent Wear
Belfast Bangor Luce Bay Wigtown Bay Workington Skiddaw 931 Ullswater Cross Fell 893
Newtownards Mull of Galloway Solway Firth Penrith Tees Barnard Castle
Sumburgh Hd. Cumbrian Mts.

SHETLAND IS.
On same scale

Unst
Fetlar
Yell Yell Sound
SHETLAND Whalsay
Mainland Bressay
Foula Scalloway Lerwick
Sumburgh Hd.

North Minch
Little Minch
Inner Hebrides
Outer Hebrides
Sound of Harris
Rubha Hunish
Trotternish
Sound of Raasay
Loch Ness
West Highlands
North West Highlands
Clyde
Firth of Clyde
North Channel

Projection: Conical with two standard parallels.
West from Greenwich
COPYRIGHT. GEORGE PHILIP & SON. LTD.

1 : 2 000 000

Towns underlined in Northern Ireland give their names to the Districts in which they stand
The remaining Districts are:—

1	Fermanagh	5	Castlereagh
2	Moyle	6	Ards
3	Newtownabbey	7	Down
4	North Down	8	Newry & Mourne

Projection: Conical with two standard parallels.

West from Greenwich

COPYRIGHT. GEORGE PHILIP & SON LTD.

50   0   50   100 miles
50   0   50   100   150 km

LITHUANIAN S.S.R.

R.S.F.S.R.

B Y E L O R U S S I A N   S.S.R.

P O L A N D

U K R A I N I A N   S.S.R.

U. S. S. R.

SLOVAKIA

HUNGARY

ROMANIA

Transilvania

MOLDAVIA

YUGOSLAVIA

BULGARIA

BLACK SEA

Zatoka Gdańska

Kaliningrad (Königsberg)
Chernyakhovsk
Vilnius
Molodechno
Borisov
Gorki
Mogilev
Krichev

Wejherowo
Gdynia
Sopot
Gdańsk (Danzig)
Elbląg
Braniewo
Gusev
Alitus
Varena
Minsk
Berezina
Bobruysk

Malbork
Lyna
Ketrzyn
Gizycko
Suwałki
Augustów
Lida
Novogrudok
Baranovichi

Kwidzyń
Olsztyn
Grodno
Mosty
Neman
Slonim
Shchara
Luninets
Gomel

Grudziądz
Mława
Ostróda
Sokółka
238
Białystok
Volkovysk
Bereza
Kalinkovichi

Chełmno
Toruń
Rypin
Lipno
Lomza
Ostrołęka
Ciechanów
Ostrów Mazowiecka
Brańsk
Hajnówka
Czeremcha
Pripyat
316
Uzh

Włocławek
Płock
Wkra
Pułtusk
Bug
Zhabinka
Brest
Dubrovitsa
Sarny
Desna

Warszawa (Warsaw)
Pruszków
Mińsk Mazowiecki
Siedlce
Biała Podlaska
Międzyrzec Podlaski
Pripyat
Korosten

Łódź
Żyrardów
Skierniewice
Grójec
Łuków
Włodawa
Kovel
Styr
Horyn
Slucz
Novograd-Volynskiy
Radomyshl
Kiyev
Borispol

Pilica
Radom
Kozienice
Puławy
Chełm
Lublin
Vladimir Volynskiy
Lutsk
Korets
Zhitomir

Kielce
Ostrowied Swietokrzysk
Sandomierz
Zamość
Sokal
Dubno
Ostrog
Shepetovka
Fastov
Belaya Tserkov

Częstochowa
Opole
Radomsko
Jędrzejów
Pinczów
Tarnobrzeg
390
Kamenka Bugskaya
Radekhov
Brody
Kremenets
Starokonstantinav
Berdichev
Kazatin

Zabrze
Bytom
Sosnowiec
Katowice
Kraków
Wieliczka
Dabrowa Tarnowska
Rzeszów
Jarosław
Przemyśl
Gorodok
Lvov
Zolochev
Khmelnitskiy
384
Vinnitsa

Bielsko-Biała
Cieszyn
Tarnów
Jasło
Nowy Sącz
Sanok
471
Sambor
Dnestr
Ternopol
Zhmerinka
Uman

Ostrava
1725
Krosno
Dukelský Pr.
502
Drogobych
Stryi
Buchach
Chortkov
Pervomaisk

Żilina
Ružomberok
2655
Prešov
Turka
Borislav
Ivano-Frankovsk
Zaleshchiki
Kamenets-Podolskiy
Bug

Nizké Tatry
Košice
Uzhgorod
Nadvornaya
1881
Kolomyya
Snyatyn
Khotin
Mogilev-Podolskiy

Kremnica
Banská Bystrica
Slovenské Rudohorie
Sátoraljaújhely
Mukachevo
Perl Yablonitse
931
Chernovtsy
Yedintsy
Soroki
Kotovsk

Nitra
Banská Štiavnica
Lučenec
Beregovo
Khust
2061
Storozhinets
Dorohoi
Beltsy

Miskolc
Bodrog
Tokaj
Satu Mare
Sighet
Radauti
Prut
429
Kishinev

Komárno
Nyíregyháza
Mezőkövesd
Carei
Baia Mare
Pietrosul
2305
Suceava
Vatra-Dornei
Botoşani
Iaşi
Bendery

Győr
Tatabánya
Esztergom
Vác
Eger
Hajdúböszörmény
Debrecen
Del
2102
Bistrita
Pietrosul
Roman
Vaslui
Bîrlad
Odessa

BUDAPEST
Újpest
Hatvan
Jászberény
Karcag
Oradea
Cluj
Turda
Tîrgu Mures
Praid
Bacău
Belgorod Dnestrovskiy

Cegléd
Nagykőrös
Mezőtúr
Salonta
1848
Abrud
Aiud
Odorhei
Miercurea Ciuc
Ozero Sasyk Kiliya

Kecskemét
Kiskunfélegyháza
Kiskőrös
Szentes
Gyula Crişul
Mtii Bihor
Alba-Iulia
Medias
Sighişoara
Bretcu

Szeged
Makó
Arad
Mures
Deva
Brad
Simleria
Sibiu
Fagaras
Braşov
Focşani
Galati
Ismail

Pécs
Mohács
Subotica
Senta
Kikinda
Timişoara
Lugoj
Hunedoara
Carpatii Meridionali
Rîmnicu Sarat
Brăila
Tulcea
Sulina

Osijek
Novi Sad
Beograd (Belgrade)
Zrenjanin (Petrovgrad)
Bečej
Caransebeş
Reşita
P. Turnu Roşu
350
Vf. Negoiu
2507
Omul
2535
Cîmpina
Ploieşti
Dunărea (Danube)

Vinkovci
Sombor
Vršac
Bela Crkva
Peleaga
2518
2509
Paringul Mare
Tîrgu-Jiu
Rîmnicu Vîlcea
Tîrgovişte
Bucureşti (Bucharest)
Constanţa

Brod
Odžak
Sremska Mitrovica
Pančevo
Porta Orientalis
Menhadia
Portile de Fier
Orsova
Turnu-Severin
Pitesti
Arges
Dîmbovita
Cernavodă
Mamaia

Bijeljina
Smederevo
Požarevac
Bela Crkva
Slatina
Craiova
Caracal
Olteniţa
Silistra
Mangalia

Tuzla
1346
Bor
Timok
Vidin
Turnu Măgurele
Zimnicea
Corabia
Giurgiu
Ruse (Ruschuk)
Tolbukhin

Sarajevo
Titovo Užice
Čačak
Zaječar
Negotin
Tom (Danube)
Vedea

1 : 5 000 000

50   0   50   100 miles
50   0   50   100   150 km

FRENCH DEPARTMENTS

A.	01	Ain
A.	02	Aisne
A.	03	Allier
A.-A.	04	Alpes-de-Haute-Provence
H.A.	05	Hautes-Alpes
A.M.	06	Alpes-Maritimes
Ard.	07	Ardèche
Ard.	08	Ardennes
Ar.	09	Ariège
Aub.	10	Aube
Aud.	11	Aude
Av.	12	Aveyron
B.Rh.	13	Bouches-du-Rhône
C.	14	Calvados
Ct.	15	Cantal
Cha.	16	Charente
Ch.M.	17	Charente-Maritime
Che.	18	Cher
Co.	19	Corrèze
C.Q.	20 a) Corse du Nord b) Corse du Sud
C.O.	21	Côte-d'Or
C.N.	22	Côtes-du-Nord
Cr.	23	Creuse
D.	24	Dordogne
Do.	25	Doubs
Dr.	26	Drôme
E.	27	Eure
E.L.	28	Eure-et-Loir
F.	29	Finistère
G.	30	Gard
H.G.	31	Haute-Garonne
Ge.	32	Gers
Gi.	33	Gironde
H.	34	Hérault
I.V.	35	Ille-et-Vilaine
I.	36	Indre
I.L.	37	Indre-et-Loire
Is.	38	Isère
J.	39	Jura
L.	40	Landes
L.C.	41	Loir-et-Cher
Lo.	42	Loire
H.L.	43	Haute-Loire
L.A.	44	Loire-Atlantique
Loi.	45	Loiret
Lot	46	Lot
L.G.	47	Lot-et-Garonne
Loz.	48	Lozère
M.L.	49	Maine-et-Loire
Ma.	50	Manche
Mar.	51	Marne
H.Ma.	52	Haute-Marne
May.	53	Mayenne
M.M.	54	Meurthe-et-Moselle
Me.	55	Meuse
Mo.	56	Morbihan
Mos.	57	Moselle
N.	58	Nièvre
No.	59	Nord
Oi.	60	Oise
Or.	61	Orne
P.C.	62	Pas-de-Calais
P.D.	63	Puy-de-Dôme
P.A.	64	Pyrénées-Atlantiques
H.P.	65	Hautes Pyrénées
P.O.	66	Pyrénées-Orientales
B.R.	67	Bas Rhin
H.R.	68	Haut Rhin
R.	69	Rhône
H.S.	70	Haute Saône
S.L.	71	Saône-et-Loire
Sa.	72	Sarthe
S.	73	Savoie
H.Sa.	74	Haute-Savoie
S.M.	76	Seine-Maritime
S.M.	77	Seine-et-Marne
D.S.	79	Deux-Sèvres
So.	80	Somme
T.	81	Tarn
T.G.	82	Tarn-et-Garonne
Va.	83	Var
Ve.	84	Vaucluse
V.	85	Vendée
Vi.	86	Vienne
H.V.	87	Haute-Vienne
Vo.	88	Vosges
Y.	89	Yonne
B.	90	Belfort
Es.	91	Essonne
H.S-D	93	Seine-St-Denis
V.O.	94	Val-de-Marne
		Val-d'Oise

CORSICA
On same scale

Corse · Haute-Corse · Corse du Sud
Calvo · Bastia · Mte. Rotondo 2625 · Corte · Porto Vecchio · Bonifacio · Ajaccio
Mt. Cinto 2710

ENGLISH CHANNEL

BAY OF BISCAY

MEDITERRANEAN SEA

BELGIUM · LUXEMBOURG · GERMANY · SWITZERLAND · ITALY · SPAIN

F R A N C E

Projection: Conical with two standard parallels

East from Greenwich

West from Greenwich

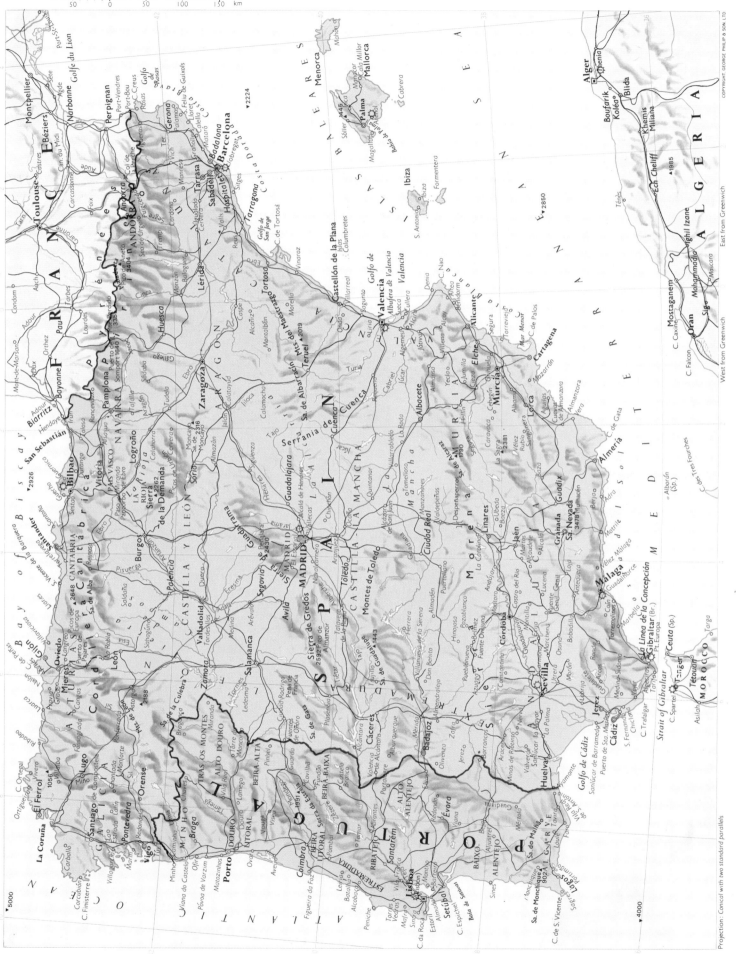

Inset

MALTA
1:1 000 000

0   5   10 miles
0   5   15 km.

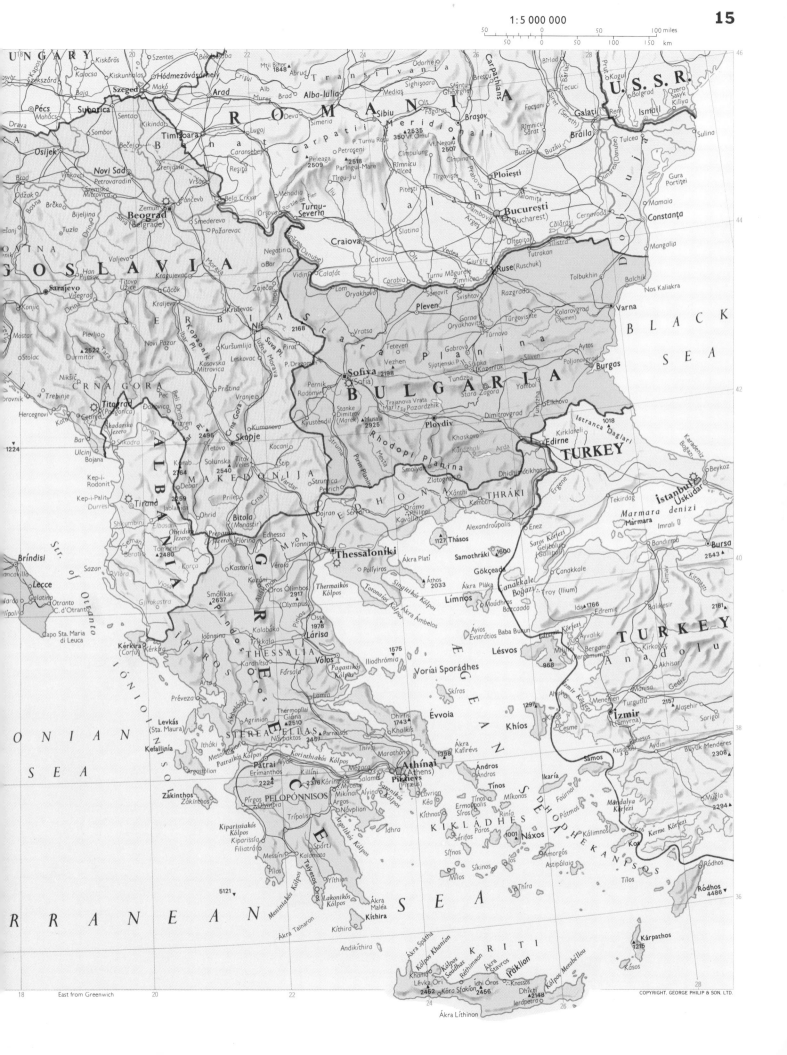

ICELAND
on the same scale
as general map

R.S.F.S.R.
1. Daghestan A.S.S.R.
2. Kabardino–Balkar A.S.S.R.
3. Mari A.S.S.R.
4. Mordovian A.S.S.R.
5. North Ossetian A.S.S.R.
6. Tatar A.S.S.R.
7. Udmurt A.S.S.R.
8. Chuvash A.S.S.R.
9. Checheno–Ingush A.S.S.R.
AZERBAIJAN
10. Nakhichevan A.S.S.R.
GEORGIA
11. Abkhaz A.S.S.R.
12. Adzhar A.S.S.R.

Projection: *Conical Orthomorphic with two standard parallels*

East from Greenwich

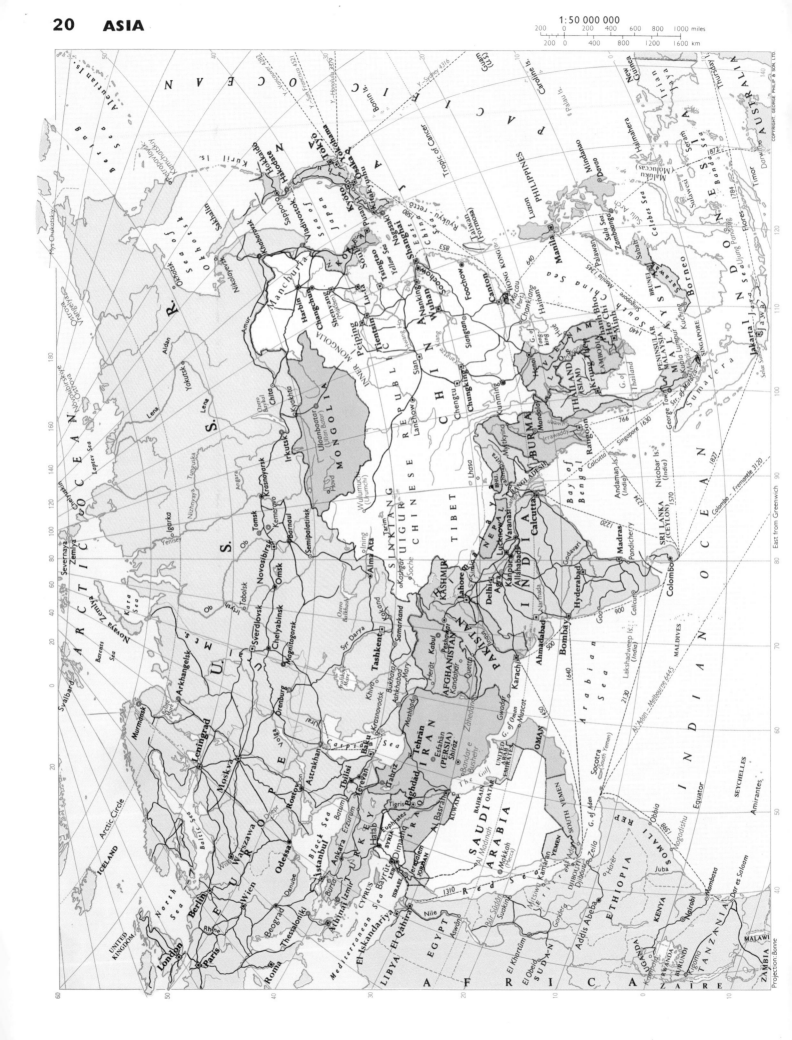

1:50 000 000

1 : 20 000 000

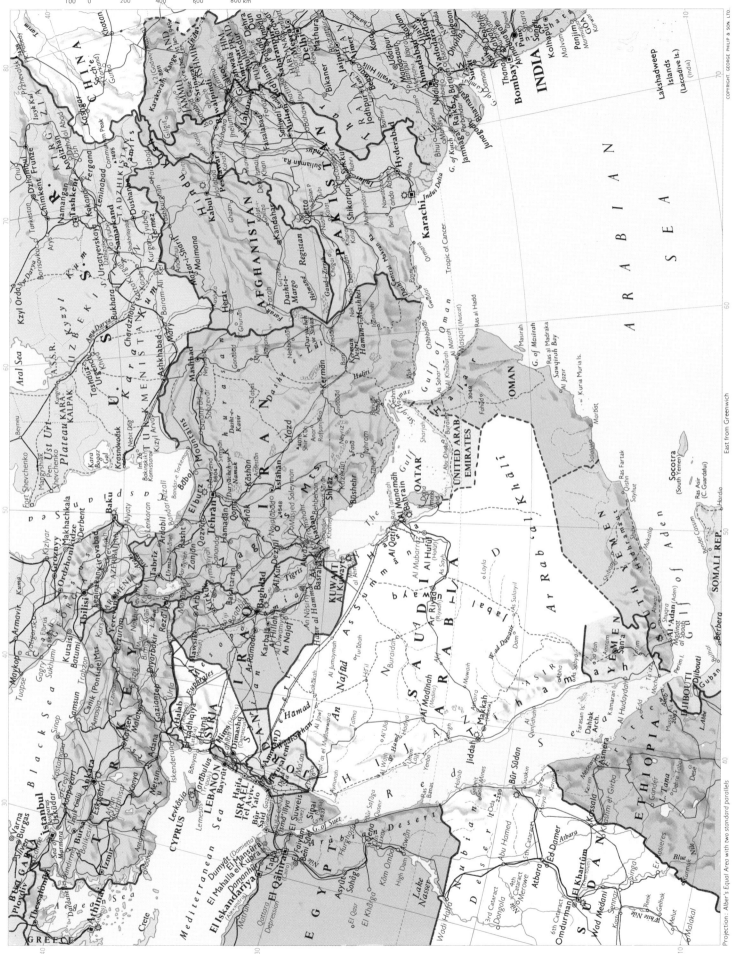

Projection: Alber's Equal Area with two standard parallels

1:20 000 000

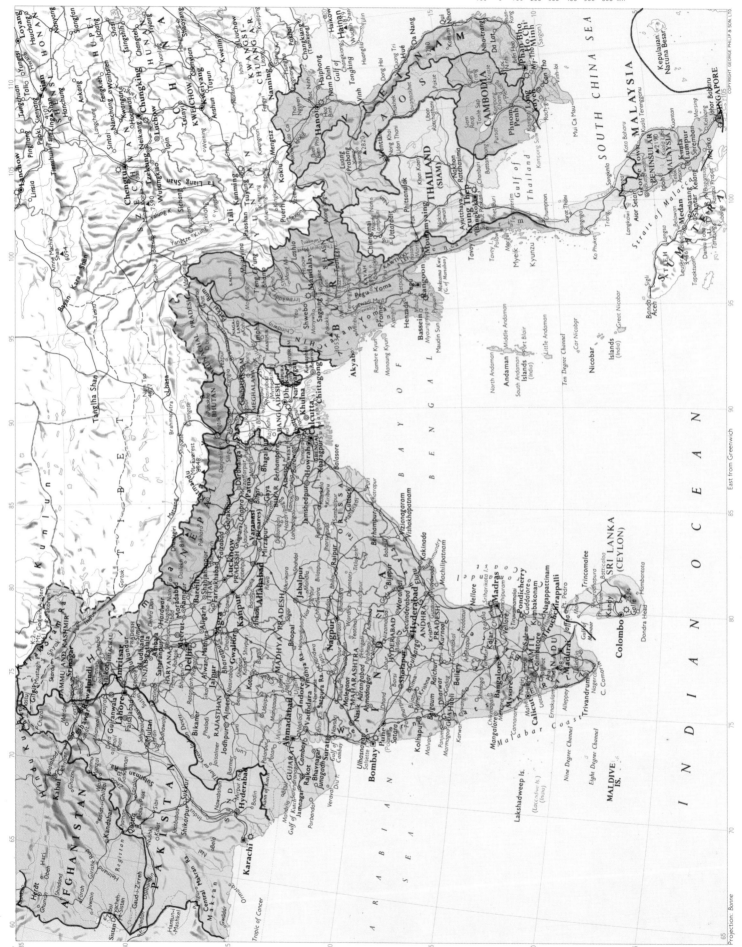

Projection: Bonne

1 : 20 000 000

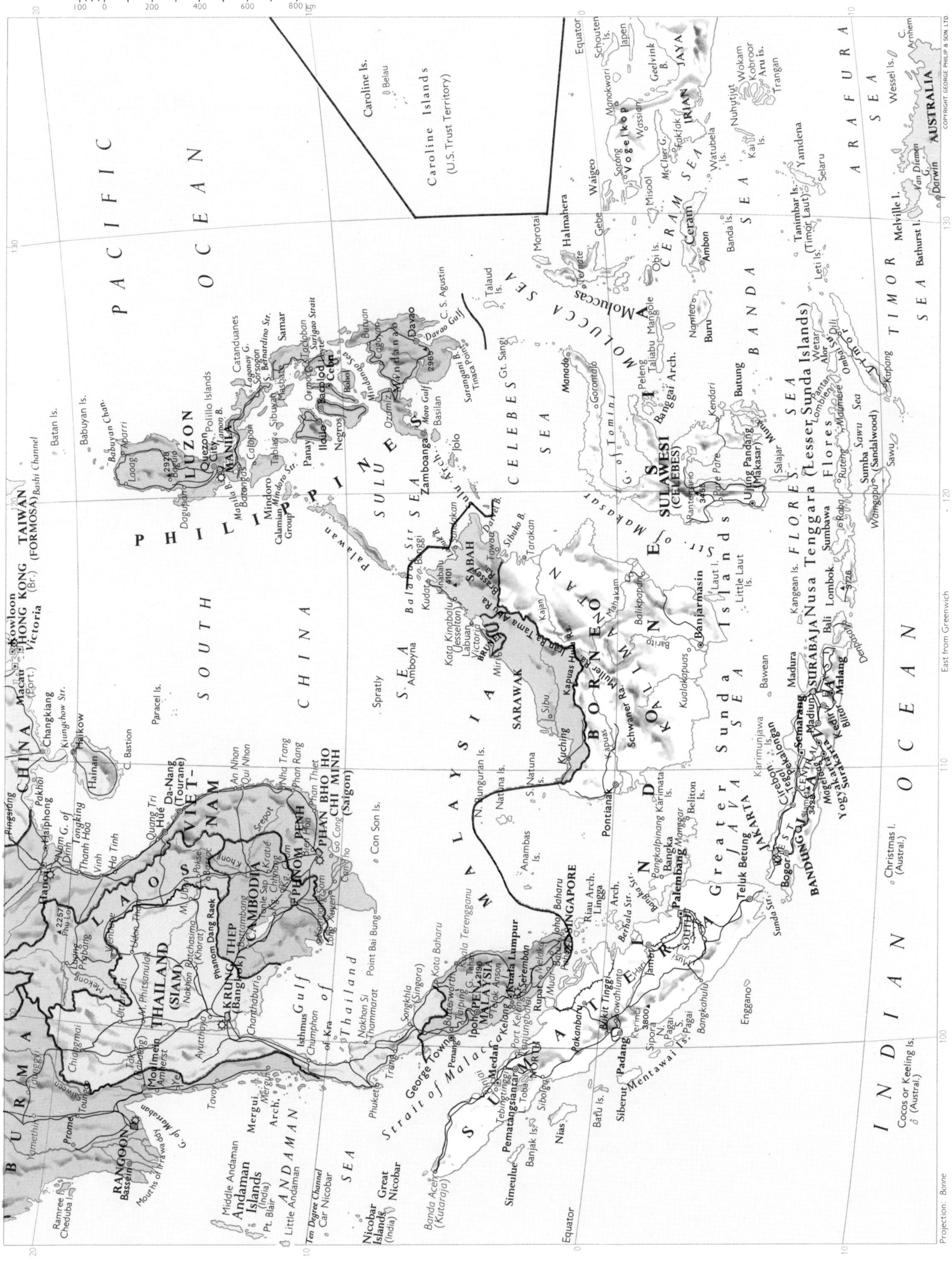

100   0   100   200   300   400   500 miles
100   0   200   400   600   800 km

Caroline Is.   Belau
Caroline Islands (U.S. Trust Territory)

P A C I F I C   O C E A N

S O U T H   C H I N A   S E A

SULU SEA

CELEBES SEA

MOLUCCA SEA

CERAM SEA

BANDA SEA

FLORES SEA

ARAFURA SEA

TIMOR SEA

JAVA SEA

ANDAMAN SEA

Gulf of Thailand

Strait of Malacca

INDIAN OCEAN

CHINA
TAIWAN (FORMOSA)
HONG KONG (Br.)
Kowloon   Victoria
Macau (Port.)
Hainan
BURMA
VIET-NAM
LAOS
THAILAND (SIAM)
CAMBODIA
KRUNG THEP (Bangkok)
PHNOM PENH
PHAN BHO HO CHI MINH (Saigon)
Hanoi   Haiphong
Da-Nang (Tourane)
Hué
RANGOON
Bassein

PHILIPPINES
LUZON
MANILA   Quezon City
MINDANAO
Davao
Cebu
Negros
Panay
Samar
Mindoro
Palawan
Zamboanga

MALAYSIA
SABAH
SARAWAK
Kota Kinabalu (Jesselton)
Kuching
SINGAPORE
Kuala Lumpur
George Town (Penang)
Ipoh
Johor Baharu
Kota Baharu

BORNEO
KALIMANTAN
Banjarmasin
Balikpapan
Pontianak

SULAWESI (CELEBES)
Ujung Pandang (Makasar)
Manado

INDONESIA
SUMATRA
JAVA
Greater Sunda Islands
Nusa Tenggara (Lesser Sunda Islands)
JAKARTA
BANDUNG
SURABAJA
Semarang
Palembang
Medan
Padang
Bali
Lombok
Sumbawa
Sumba (Sandalwood)
Flores
Timor
Madura

IRIAN JAYA
Halmahera
Buru
Ambon

AUSTRALIA
Darwin
Melville I.
Bathurst I.

Andaman Islands (India)
Nicobar Islands (India)
Cocos or Keeling Is. (Austral.)
Christmas I. (Austral.)

Spratly
Paracel Is.
Natuna Is.
Anambas Is.

Equator

East from Greenwich

Projection: Bonne

SEA OF JAPAN

CHŪGOKU

SHIKOKU

KYŪSHŪ

PACIFIC OCEAN

KINKI

TŌKAIDO LINE

SOUTH KOREA

Sea of Okhotsk

HOKKAIDO

TŌHOKU

KANTŌ

CHŪBU

East from Greenwich

1:5 000 000

25 0 25 50 75 100 miles
25 0 50 100 150 km
Projection: Conical with two standard parallels

East from Greenwich

1:10 000 000

100 50 0 50 100 150 200 miles
100 0 100 200 300 km
Projection: Bonne

Continuation Southwards on same scale

Ōsumi-Shotō 1935
Tane-ga-Shima
Yaku-Shima
Tokara-Kaikyō
Tokara-Shima
Suwanose-Jima
Nansei-Shotō
Amami-Ō-Shima
Toku-no-Shima

REFERENCE TO PREFECTURES

HOKKAIDO DISTRICT		KINKI DISTRICT	
1	Hokkaidō	24	Hyogo
TŌHOKU DISTRICT		25	Kyōto
2	Aomori	26	Shiga
3	Akita	27	Ōsaka
4	Iwate	28	Nara
5	Yamagata	29	Mie
6	Miyagi	30	Wakayama
7	Fukushima	**CHŪGOKU DISTRICT**	
CHŪBU DISTRICT		31	Tottori
8	Niigata	32	Okayama
9	Ishikawa	33	Shimane
10	Toyama	34	Hiroshima
11	Fukui	35	Yamaguchi
12	Gifu	**SHIKOKU DISTRICT**	
13	Nagano	36	Kagawa
14	Yamanashi	37	Tokushima
15	Aichi	38	Ehime
16	Shizuoka	39	Kōchi
KANTŌ DISTRICT		**KYŪSHŪ DISTRICT**	
17	Gumma	40	Fukuoka
18	Tochigi	41	Saga
19	Saitama	42	Nagasaki
20	Ibaraki	43	Kumamoto
21	Tōkyō	44	Ōita
22	Chiba	45	Miyazaki
23	Kanagawa	46	Kagoshima

1:20 000 000

100 0 100 200 300 400 miles
100 0 100 200 300 400 500 600 km

U. S. S. R.

UNION OF SOVIET SOCIALIST REPUBLICS

KAZAKH S.S.R.

KIRGIZ S.S.R.

M O N G O L I A

MONGOLIAN REPUBLIC

INNER MONGOLIA

Ulaanbaatar (Ulan Bator)

Ulan Ude

Irkutsk

Chita

Khabarovsk

Vladivostok

HARBIN

SHENYANG

NORTH KOREA

Pyongyang

SOUTH KOREA

Seoul

Pusan

JAPAN

Fukuoka

Nagasaki

PEIPING (Peking)

TIENTSIN

TAIYUAN

Paotow

Huhehot

Tatung

Changkiakow

SHANSI

HOPEI

SHANTUNG

Tsingtao

YELLOW SEA

SHANGHAI

NANKING

Soochow

Hangchow

CHEKIANG

Wenchow

Hankow

WUHAN

HUPEH

HUNAN

Changsha

KIANGSI

Nanchang

FUKIEN

Foochow

TAIWAN (Formosa)

Taipei

Kaohsiung

EAST CHINA SEA

Ryukyu-retto

Tropic of Cancer

KWANGTUNG

Canton

HONG KONG

Macau

Kowloon

Victoria

KWANGSI

Nanning

KWEICHOW

Kweiyang

YUNNAN

Kunming

SZECHWAN

CHUNGKING

CHENGTU

TsINGHAI

Sining

KANSU

Lanchow

Yinchwan

NINGSIA

Ala Shan

Ordos

GREAT WALL

SHENSI

SIAN

HONAN

Chengchow

Kaifeng

Loyang

ANHWEI

Hwainan

KIANGSU

Hefei

SINKIANG-UIGUR
(Autonomous Region)

Wulumuchi

Dzungaria

Tarim

Takla Makan

Kashgar

T I B E T
(Autonomous Region)

Lhasa

Tangla Shan

Nyenchen Tangla Shan

SOUTH CHINA SEA

BURMA

Mandalay

Rangoon

THAILAND (SIAM)

LAOS

VIETNAM

Hanoi

Haiphong

G. of Tongking

NEPAL

Katmandu

BHUTAN

BANGLADESH

Dacca

I N D I A

Calcutta

Howrah

Patna

Lucknow

Varanasi

Allahabad

Kanpur

JAMMU & KASHMIR

BAY OF BENGAL

Vishakhapatnam

PHILIPPINES

Luzon

Manila

Laoag

East from Greenwich

Projection: Bonne

Boundaries of the artesian basins --------

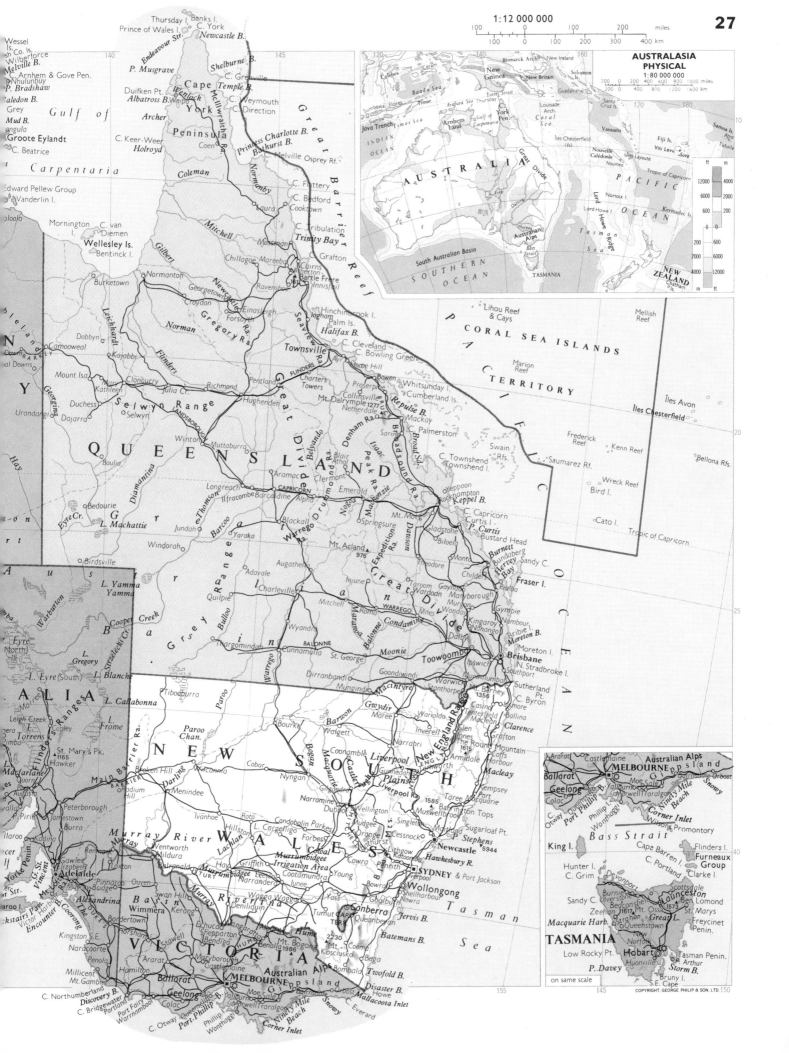

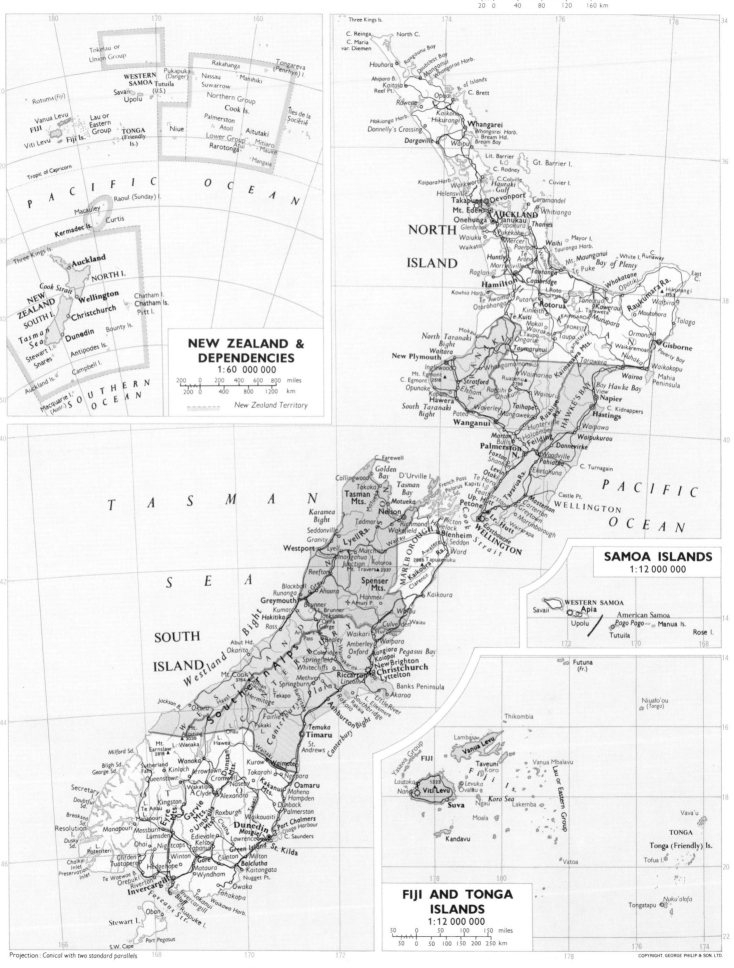

1:6 000 000

NEW ZEALAND & DEPENDENCIES

1:60 000 000

New Zealand Territory

SAMOA ISLANDS

1:12 000 000

FIJI AND TONGA ISLANDS

1:12 000 000

Projection: Conical with two standard parallels

COPYRIGHT. GEORGE PHILIP & SON, LTD.

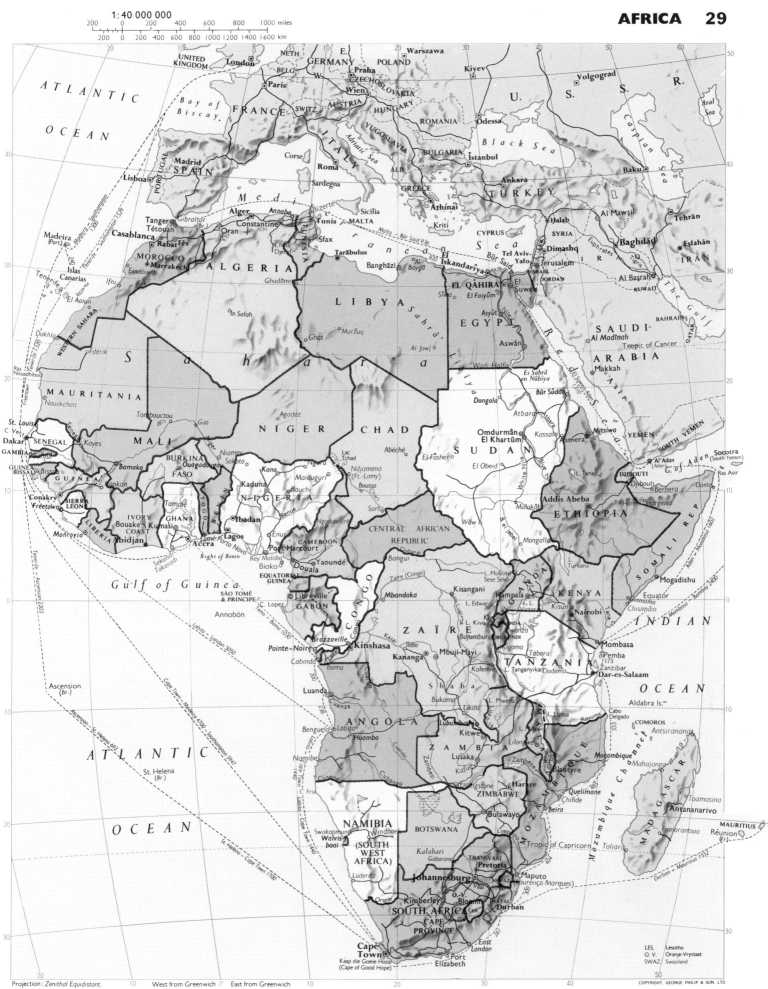

1:40 000 000

200   0   200   400   600   800   1000 miles
200 0 200 400 600 800 1000 1200 1400 1600 km

ATLANTIC OCEAN

UNITED KINGDOM
London
NETH.
BELG.
GERMANY
POLAND
Warszawa
Kiyev
Volgograd
Aral Sea
Bay of Biscay
FRANCE
Paris
Praha
CZECHOSLOVAKIA
Wien
AUSTRIA
HUNGARY
ROMANIA
Odessa
U.   S.   S.   R.
SWITZ.
ITALY
YUGOSLAVIA
Black Sea
İstanbul
Baku
Caspian Sea
Madeira (Port.)
Madrid
SPAIN
Lisboa
PORTUGAL
Corse
Roma
Adriatic Sea
BULGARIA
Ankara
TURKEY
Tehrān
Islas Canarias
Tenerife
El Aaiun
Tanger
Tétouan
Casablanca
Rabat
Fès
MOROCCO
Marrakech
Essaouira
Ifni
Oran
Alger
Constantine
Annaba
Bizerte
TUNISIA
Tunis
MALTA
Sicilia
Sardegna
Mediterranean Sea
GREECE
Athínai
Kriti
CYPRUS
SYRIA
Halab
Dimashq
Tel Aviv-Yafo
Jerusalem
ISRAEL
JORDAN
Al Mawşil
Baghdād
Eşfahān
IRAN
Al Başrah
KUWAIT
BAHRAIN
QATAR
SAUDI-ARABIA
Al Madīnah
Makkah
Tarābulus
Banghāzi
El Bayda
Bûr Said 936
El Iskandariya
El Qāhira
El Faiyûm
El Suweis
EGYPT
Siwa
Asyût
Aswân
Wadi Halfa
Tropic of Cancer
Fdérik
WESTERN SAHARA
Dakhla
S a h a r a
In Salah
Ghudâmis
Ghat
Marzuq
Al Jawf
LIBYA
Es Sahrâ en Nûbiya
Wadi Halfa
Nouakchott
MAURITANIA
Ras Nouadhibou
NIGER
CHAD
SUDAN
Dongola
Bûr Sûdan
Atbara
Port Sudan
YEMEN
SOUTH YEMEN
Socotra (South Yemen)
Ras Asir
G. of Aden
Al'Adan (Aden)
Berbera
Hargeisa
Danto
SOMALI REP.
MALI
Tombouctou
Gao
Agadez
Ndjamena (Ft.-Lamy)
Lac Tchad
Abéché
El Fasher
El Obeid
Omdurmân
El Khartûm
Kassala
Asmera
Mitsiwa
DJIBOUTI
Djibouti
L. Tana
Addis Abeba
Harer
ETHIOPIA
SENEGAL
St. Louis
C. Vert
Dakar
GAMBIA
Banjul
GUINEA BISSAU
Bissau
Conakry
Freetown
SIERRA LEONE
LIBERIA
Monrovia
GUINEA
Kankan
Bamako
Kayes
BURKINA FASO
Ouagadougou
Niamey
Sokoto
Kano
Kaduna
Maiduguri
Nguru
Bauchi
NIGERIA
Ibadan
Lagos
Benue
CAMEROON
Ngaoundéré
Yaoundé
Douala
EQUATORIAL GUINEA
Bioko
SÃO TOMÉ & PRINCIPE
C. Lopez
GABON
Libreville
Annobón
CONGO
Brazzaville
Pointe-Noire
Cabinda
Kinshasa
Boma
Luanda
Cuanza
ANGOLA
Benguela
Lobito
Huambo
Namibe
IVORY COAST
Bouaké
Tamale
GHANA
TOGO
BENIN
Kumasi
Abidjan
Sekondi-Takoradi
Bight of Benin
Accra
Lomé
Porto Novo
Rey Malabo
Port Harcourt
Enugu
Gulf of Guinea
ATLANTIC OCEAN
Ascension (Br.)
St. Helena (Br.)
CENTRAL AFRICAN REPUBLIC
Bangui
Oubangi
Zaire (Congo)
Mbandaka
Kisangani
ZAÏRE
Ilebo
Kananga
Mbuji-Mayi
Kasai
UGANDA
Kampala
L. Mobutu Sese Seko
L. Edward
L. Kivu
RWANDA
Bujumbura
BURUNDI
KENYA
Nairobi
L. Turkana
L. Victoria
Kisumu
Mombasa
Equator
INDIAN OCEAN
TANZANIA
Dodoma
Dar-es-Salaam
Zanzibar
Pemba
Tabora
L. Tanganyika
Kalemie
Kigoma
Bukama
Shaba
Likasi
Lubumbashi
Kitwe
L. Mweru
L. Nyasa
COMOROS
Antsiranana
Cabo Delgado
Ravuma
Lilongwe
MALAWI
Blantyre
ZAMBIA
Lusaka
Kafue
Kabwe
Zambezi
MOZAMBIQUE
Moçambique
Quelimane
Chinde
Beira
Mahajanga
MADAGASCAR
Toamasina
Antananarivo
Fianarantsoa
Toliara
MAURITIUS
Réunion (Fr.)
Harare
ZIMBABWE
Bulawayo
Limpopo
NAMIBIA (SOUTH WEST AFRICA)
Windhoek
Swakopmund
Walvis-baai
Lüderitz
Kalahari
BOTSWANA
Gaborone
Tropic of Capricorn
TRANSVAAL
Pretoria
Johannesburg
SWAZ.
Maputo (Lourenço Marques)
Kimberley
O.V.
Bloemfontein
LES.
NATAL
Durban
Vaal
Oranje
SOUTH AFRICA
CAPE PROVINCE
Cape Town
Kaap die Goeie Hoop (Cape of Good Hope)
East London
Port Elizabeth

Projection: Zenithal Equidistant.   West from Greenwich   East from Greenwich

LES. Lesotho
O. V. Oranje-Vrystaat
SWAZ. Swaziland

COPYRIGHT. GEORGE PHILIP & SON. LTD.

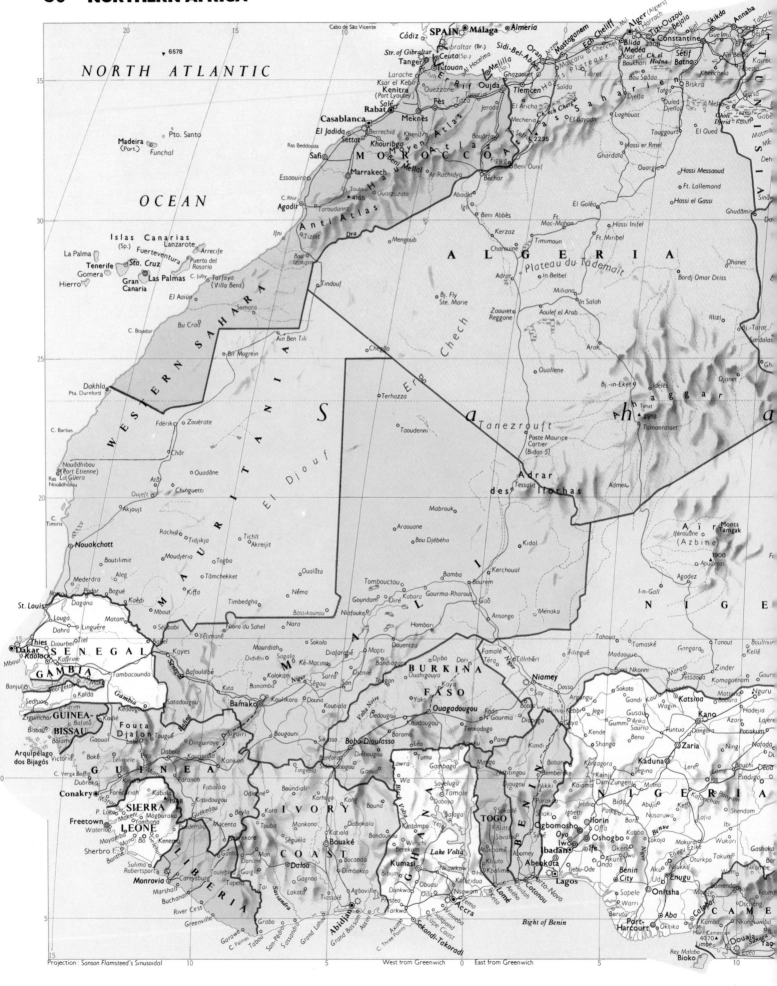

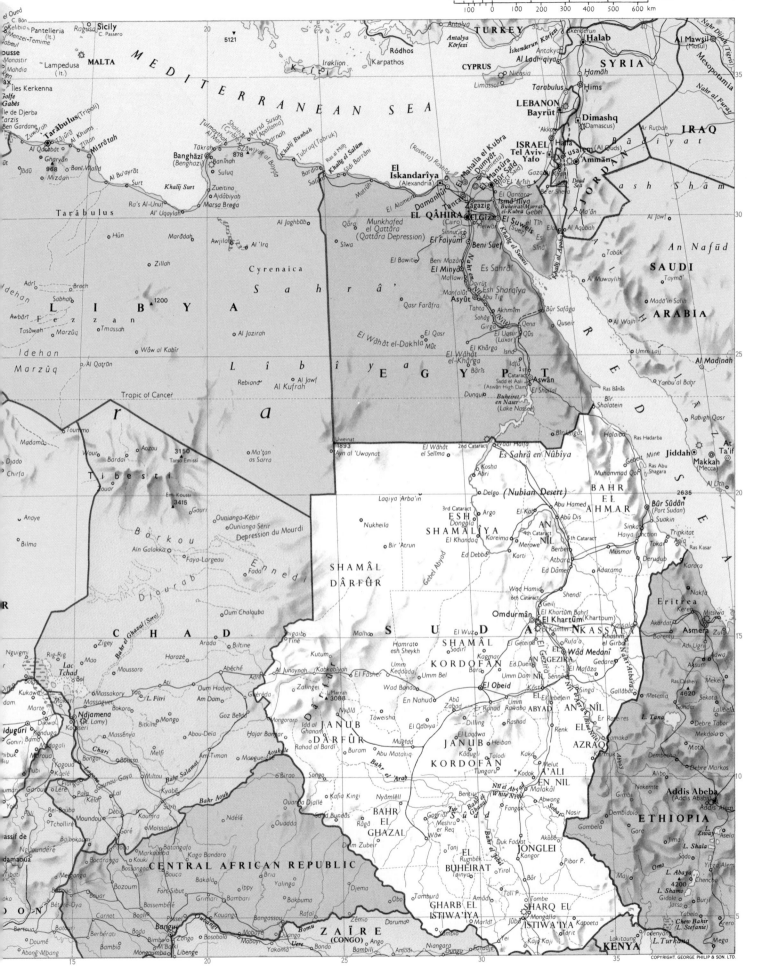

1:15 000 000

100   0   100   200   300   400 miles
100   0   100   200   300   400   500   600 km

MEDITERRANEAN SEA

C. Bōn
Pantelleria (It.)
Ragusa **Sicily** C. Passero
Menzel-Temime
Mahdia Lampedusa (It.) **MALTA**
Sfax Iles Kerkenna
Golfe
Gabès
Ile de Djerba
Zarzis
Ben Gardane
Zuwarah
Tarābulus (Tripoli)
Tājūrā Al Khums
Al Qabāt Zlitan **Misrātah**
Gharyān
Jādū Beni Walid
968 Surt
Mizdah
L I B Y A
Tarābulus
Khalīj Surt

Rōdhos
Kríti Iraklion Karpathos
Antalya Antalya Körfezi
TURKEY
İskenderun Körfezi Al Mawşil (Mosul)
Nahr Dijla (Tigris)
Nicasia Antakya **Halab**
CYPRUS Al Lādhiqiya **SYRIA**
Limassol Hamāh
Tarābulus Ḥims
LEBANON
Bayrūt Ar Rutbah **IRAQ**
Akko Dimashq (Damascus) Bādiyat
Haifa Jerusalem (Al Quds) **Ammān** ash Shām
ISRAEL Ammān **JORDAN**
Tel Aviv-Yafo
Gaza Be'er Sheba
Dead Sea Ma'ān
El 'Arish
El Qantara Al Jawf
Ismâ'ilîya
Būr Said (Port Said) Al Aqabah
Es Suweis (Suez) Elat
El Tih Tabūk **SAUDI**
Gebel Sīnâ'
Khalīj el Suweis Al Muwaylih **ARABIA**
Taymā'
An Nafūd

Tūkrah Susah Apollonia
Shaḥḥat (Cyrene) Marsā Susah
878 Al Marj Darnah
Banghāzi (Benghazi) Banīnah Khalīj Bunbah
Suluq Tubruq (Tobruk) Ras al Hilāl
Ajdābiyah Bardia Sīdi Barrāni
Zueitina Salūm
Marsa Brega Marsā Maţrūh El 'Alamein Damanhûr
Al 'Uqaylah El Iskandarîya (Alexandria) Tanta
968 Qārā El Qâhira (Cairo) Zagazig
Hūn Maradah Siwa El Giza El Suweis
Awjilah Al Jaghbūb Munkhafad Helwân
Zillah Al 'Iraq el Qattāra El Falyūm
(Qattâra Depression) Beni Suef
El Bawiti Beni Mazār
El Minyā Es Sahrā'
Mallawi
Manfalūt Esh Sharqîya
Cyrenaica Qasr Faráfra Asyût An Tig
Akhmîm
S a h r ā ' Tahta Nag' Hammâdi Sohāg Qena Qūs
El Wâhât el-Dakhla Girga El Uqsur (Luxor)
Mūt El Qasr El Khârga Isna Qūseir
El Wâhât Idfū Būr Safâga
L i b y a n el-Khârga Bāris 1st Qena
Cataract Aswân
E G Y P T Sadd el Aali El Shallal
(Aswân High Dam)
Dunqul
Buheiret Ras Bânās
en Naser Bir
(Lake Nasser) Shalatein

Adrī Brach
Sabhā Al Qaţrūn
Tasāwah Marzūq
Awbāri Tmassah Rebiana
F e z z a n Al Jawf
Wāw al Kabīr Al Kufrah
Marzūq
Idehan
Mārzūq
Tropic of Cancer

Al Jazirah Al Wāhāt el Selima 2nd Cataract Wadi Halfa
1200 El Qasr **Es Sahrā en Nûbîya**
Ayn al 'Uwaynat Būr 'Unqât
Uweinat Halaiba
1893 Ras Hadarba
Kosha
Abri Mine **Jiddah**
Muhammad Qôr At Ta'if
Delgo Shagara
Halaib **Makkah** (Mecca)

Taymā'
ARABIA
Madā'in Sālih
Al Wajh
Umm Lajj
25
Al Madīnah
Yanbu'al Bahr
Rabigh Qasr
At Ta'if
Al Lith
Makkah (Mecca)
20
2635

Tibesti
Toummo
Madama Aozou
Wour Bardai
Djado Tarso Emissi 3150
Chirfa Zouar Emi Koussi 3415
Anaye Gouri
Bilma Ma'tan as Sarra
Laqiya Arba'in
Nukheila
Bir 'Atrun

3rd Cataract Argo
ESH Dongola
SHAMÂLÎYA El Kab
El Khandaq Kareima Abū Dis Abū Hamed
(Nubian Desert) 4th Cataract **BAHR**
Ed Debba Abū Dom 5th Cataract **EL**
Merowe Korti Berber **AHMAR** Būr Sūdān (Port Sudan)
Ed Dâmer Sinkat Suakin
AN Atbara Haiya Junction Trinkitat
NIL Tokar Aqiq
Shendi Musmar Ras Kasar
6th Cataract Derudeb Karora

B o r k o u
Ounianga-Kébir
Aozou Ounianga Sérir
Gouro **Depression du Mourdi**
Faya-Largeau Fada
E n n e d i
Oum Chalouba

S H A M Â L
D Â R F Û R
Gebel Abyad

Eritrea
Nakfa
Kassala Keren Mitsiwa
El Khartûm Bahrî Zula
Omdurmán **El Khartûm** (Khartoum) Akordat **Asmera**
Geili Kassala Adi Ugri
Wad Hamid **A N** Khashm Barentu
N I L el Girba Adwa Aksum
Ad Dâmer **NKASSALA** Mekele
S U D A N
El Geteina Rufa'a Gedaref 4620
SHAMÂL **El Wâd Medanî** Metemma Sekota
KORDOFAN **EL** Gallábat L. Tana Gonder Lalibela
Sodirî Ed Dueim **GEZIRA** El Mafâza
Kagmar Sennâr Debre Tabor
Umm Keddada Umm Bel Abū Zabad **AN** El Fau **NÎL** Mota
En Nahud Er Rahad **NÎL** El Mekela
EL **AZRAQ** Dembecha
Debre Markos

CHAD
Zigey
Rig-Rig Mao
Moussoro Arada Biltine
Ati Abéché
Oum Hadjer Am Dam Adré
Bokoro Guéréda
Bitkine Mongo
Massénya
Melfi

Iriba Tiné
Kutum Malha
Hamrat **SHAMÂL**
esh Sheikh **KORDOFAN**
Kabkâbîya El Fasher Umm Keddada
Junaynah (El Junaynah)
Zalingei Mêllit 3088
Nyâlâ Umm Bel
Mongororo Tâweisha El Odaiya Dilling
Goz Beïda **Idd al** Rashad Heiban
JANUB Ghanam Muglad
Hajar Banga **DÂRFÛR** Rahad al Bardî Abū Matâriq Kâdugli Talodi Kaka
Am-Timan Buram Tungaru Kodok Melut
Birao Songo **JANUB** A'ALI
Nyâmlêll **KORDOFAN** **EN NIL**

Lac Tchad
Kukawa
Ndjamena (Fort Lamy)
Koussèri
Massakory
Bokoro
Chari
Bongor
Bousso
Laï

Kafia Kingi Nyâmlêll
Ouanda Djallé Râga Bentiu
Dâm Zubeir Meshra Malakal
Ndélé **BAHR** er Req **White Nile**
Ouadda **EL** Tonj Waw Fangak Nasir
GHAZAL Gogrial Sobat
CENTRAL AFRICAN REPUBLIC
Bria Yalinga **EL** Duk Fadiat Akôbo
Bakala **BUHEIRAT** Yirol **JONGLEI**
Bambari **Rumbek** Bôr Pibor P.
Bakouma Tali P.
Djema Amâdi Tombe
ETHIOPIA
Addis Alem **Addis Abeba** (Addis Ababa)
Gimbi
Gore Ghimbi
Dembidolo Gambela
L. Tana
Gore
Ziwai L. Ziway
L. Shala
Sodo
L. Abaya 4200
L. Shamo Chencha
Gidole Burji
Yitea Alem Asela

Bangui **ZAÏRE (CONGO)**
Mongoumba Libenge
GHARB EL **SHARQ EL**
ISTIWA'IYA **ISTIWA'IYA**
Marídi Jūba
Yambio Mongalla
Dungu Kapoeta
Niangara Loka
KENYA
L. Turkana
Chew Bahir (L. Stefanie)
L. Shamo

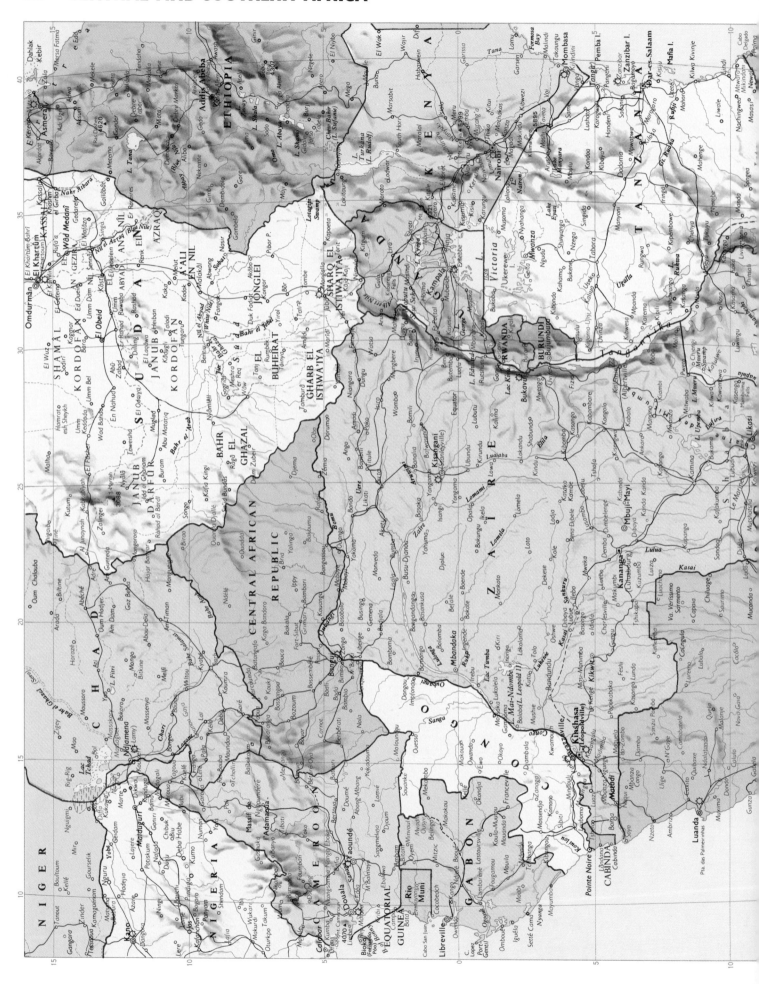

1:15 000 000

100 0 100 200 300 400 miles.
100 0 100 200 300 400 500 600 km

MADAGASCAR
On same scale as General Map
COPYRIGHT GEORGE PHILIP & SON, LTD.

INDIAN OCEAN

INDIAN OCEAN

Tropic of Capricorn

ATLANTIC OCEAN

ZIMBABWE

BOTSWANA

Kalahari

NAMIBIA
(SOUTH WEST AFRICA)

Namaland

Damaraland

Namib Desert

TRANSVAAL

Pretoria

Johannesburg

ORANJE-VRYSTAAT
(O.V.S.)

LESOTHO

SWAZILAND

NATAL

Durban

CAPE PROVINCE

SOUTH AFRICA

Cape Town

Kimberley

Bloemfontein

Port Elizabeth

East London

Windhoek

Walvisbaai

Gaborone

Bulawayo

Harare

Lusaka

Beira

Maputo (Lourenço Marques)

Blantyre

L. Nyasa (Malawi)

Pietermaritzburg

Victoria Falls

Livingstone

Okavango Swamps

Caprivi Strip

Etosha Pan

Cape of Good Hope

Tropic of Capricorn

East from Greenwich

Projection: Sanson Flamsteed's Sinusoidal

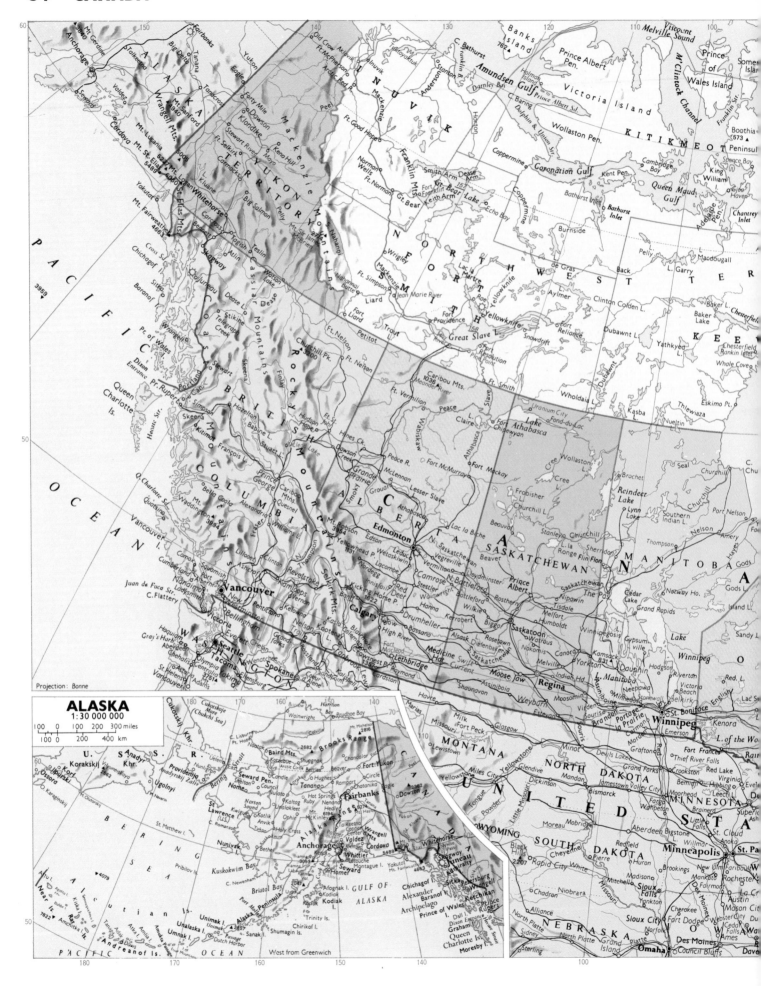

Projection: Bonne

ALASKA
1:30 000 000
100   0   100 200 300 miles
100   0   200   400 km

1:15 000 000

West from Greenwich

COPYRIGHT GEORGE PHILIP & SON, LTD.

HAWAII
1:10 000 000
20 0 20 40 60 80 miles
20 0 40 80 120 km

Projection: Albers' Equal Area with two standard parallels

1:12 000 000

50   0   50   100   150   200   250   300 miles
50 0 50 100 150 200 250 300 350 400 450 km

C A N A D A

Lake Winnipeg

Berens

Trout Lake L. St. Joseph

English L. Seul

Winnipeg

Kenora

Lake of the Wood

Thief River Falls

Red Lake

Bemidji Hibbing Virginia

MINNESOTA Duluth Superior

Moorhead

Leech L.

Brainerd

St. Cloud

Minneapolis St. Paul

WISCONSIN

Madison Milwaukee Racine

Kenosha

IOWA

Des Moines

Council Bluffs

Davenport Rock Island

Dubuque

Rockford CHICAGO

Gary

MISSOURI

Kansas City St. Louis

Springfield

Tulsa

OKLAHOMA CITY

Fort Smith

ARKANSAS Little Rock

Hot Springs

Dallas

Shreveport

Fort Worth

LOUISIANA

Baton Rouge

Houston Pasadena

Galveston

New Orleans

Delta of the Mississippi

GULF OF MEXICO

Lake Superior

Thunder Bay (Ft. William, Port Arthur)

Michipicoten I.

Sault Ste. Marie

Lake Michigan

Lake Huron

Georgian Bay

TORONTO

Hamilton Niagara Falls Buffalo

Rochester

Detroit Lake Erie

Toledo Cleveland Akron Youngstown

Grand Rapids Lansing Flint

Milwaukee

ILLINOIS INDIANA OHIO

Peoria Indianapolis Dayton Columbus

Cincinnati

Terre Haute

Evansville Louisville Lexington

KENTUCKY

Nashville

TENNESSEE

Memphis

Chattanooga

Knoxville

Birmingham

Atlanta

ALABAMA GEORGIA

Montgomery Columbus

Mobile

Pensacola

Tallahassee

FLORIDA

Jacksonville

Orlando

Tampa St. Petersburg

Miami

Key West

MONTRÉAL

Ottawa

Québec

MAINE

NEW BRUNSWICK

Bangor

St. Lawrence

VERMONT

NEW HAMPSHIRE

Boston

MASS.

CONN. R.I.

New York

PENNSYLVANIA

Pittsburgh

Philadelphia

Baltimore

Washington D.C.

WEST VIRGINIA

VIRGINIA

Richmond

Norfolk

NORTH CAROLINA

Raleigh

Charlotte Greensboro

SOUTH CAROLINA

Columbia

Charleston

Savannah

ATLANTIC OCEAN

BAHAMAS

Grand Bahama I.

Gt. Abaco

Eleuthera I.

N.W. Providence Channel

COPYRIGHT. GEORGE PHILIP & SON. LTD

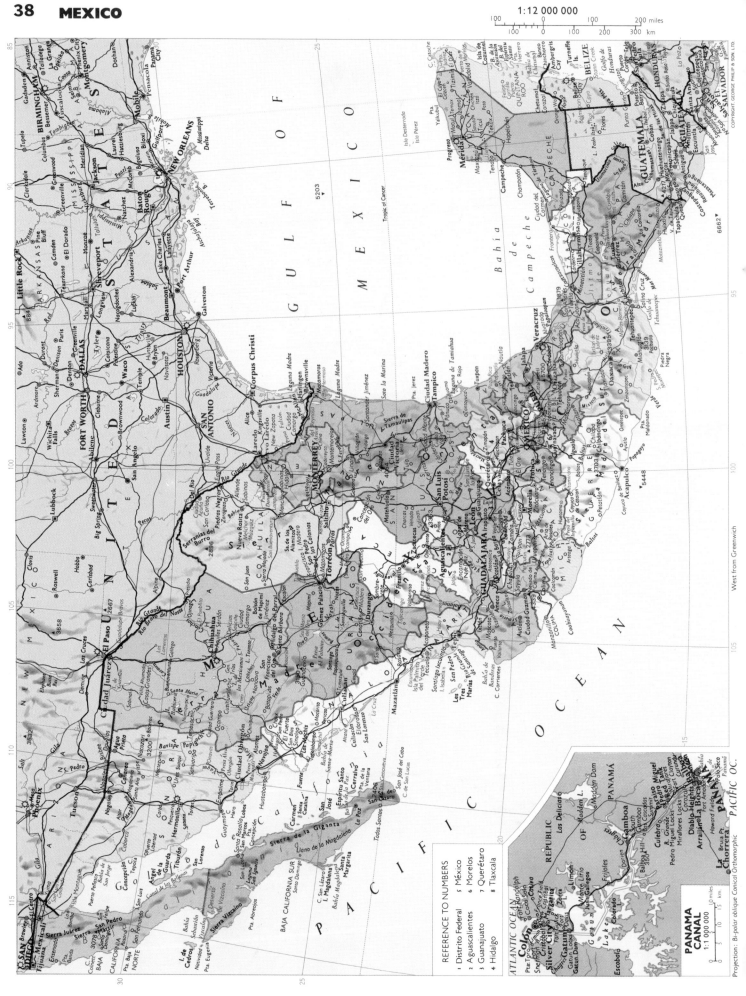

1:12 000 000

REFERENCE TO NUMBERS

1 Distrito Federal   5 México
2 Aguascalientes   6 Morelos
3 Guanajuato   7 Querétaro
4 Hidalgo   8 Tlaxcala

PANAMA CANAL
1:1 000 000

Projection: Bi-polar oblique Conical Orthomorphic

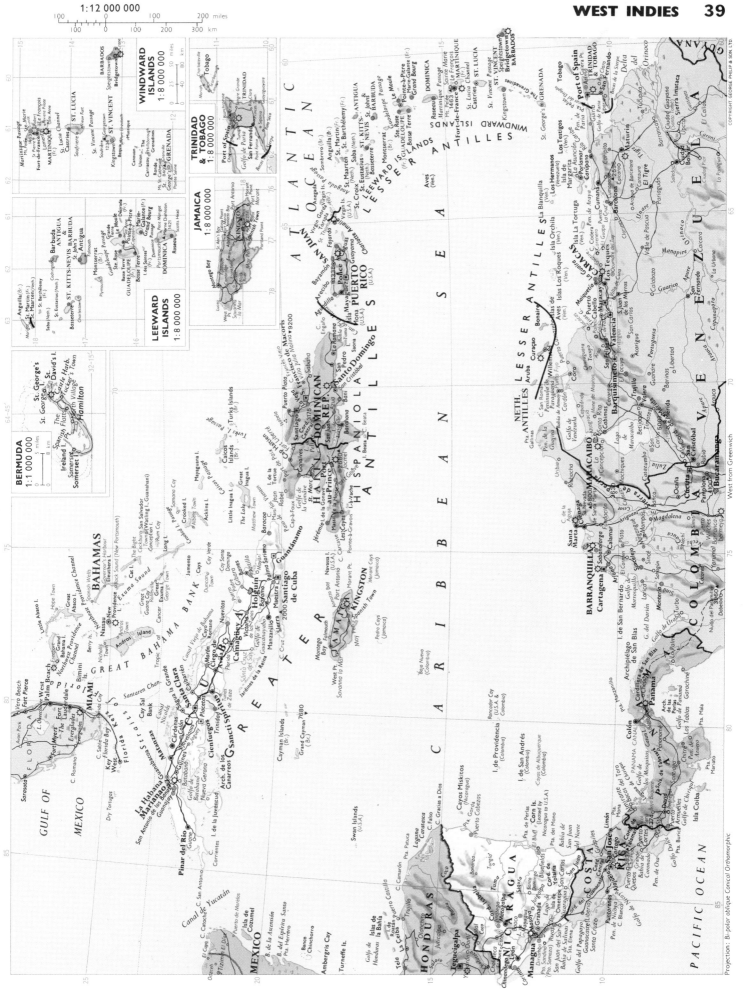

1:12 000 000

100   0   100   200 miles
100   0   100   200   300 km

WINDWARD ISLANDS
1:8 000 000

TRINIDAD & TOBAGO
1:8 000 000

JAMAICA
1:8 000 000

LEEWARD ISLANDS
1:8 000 000

BERMUDA
1:1 000 000

ATLANTIC OCEAN

GULF OF MEXICO

BAHAMAS

GREAT BAHAMA BANK

C A R I B B E A N   S E A

LESSER ANTILLES

G R E A T E R   A N T I L L E S

CUBA

JAMAICA

HAITI

DOMINICAN REP.

HISPANIOLA

PUERTO RICO (U.S.A.)

WINDWARD ISLANDS

LEEWARD ISLANDS

MEXICO

HONDURAS

NICARAGUA

COSTA RICA

PANAMA

COLOMBIA

VENEZUELA

PACIFIC OCEAN

West from Greenwich

Projection: Bi-polar oblique Conical Orthomorphic

1:16 000 000

100   0   100   200   300   400   500 miles
100   0   100   200   300   400   500   600   700   800 km

ATLANTIC

Amsterdam
Nickerie
Totness
Paramaribo
Nieuw Amsterdam
RINAM
Moengo Mana Iracoubo
Albina St. Laurent Sinnamary Kourou
Brokopondo Cayenne
wakaegron
FR.
GUIANA
St. Georges Oiapoque
C. Orange
Approuague
Kaw
Camopi
Serra
Tumucumaque
Oiapoque

AMAPÁ
Amapá
C. do Norte
Araguari
Serra
do Navio Sta. Grande
Macapá
Estuario do
Rio Amazonas
Ilha Caviana
Ilha Mexiana
Ilha de
Marajó
Ilha Maguarinho

Equator

ATLANTIC

Meriruma
Mazagão
Afuá Chaves
I. Grande
de Gurupá
Monte Alegre Gurupá Breves Muaná Curuçá Galinópolis
Prainha Almeirim Souré Vigia Bragança
Óbidos Porto de Moz Jacundá Baião Viseu
Santarém Almeirim Cametá Belém (Pará) Guimarães Turiaçu B. de São Marcos São Luís (Maranhão) Barreirinhas
Belterra Curralinho Abaetetuba Acará Alcântara Tutoia Luís Correia
Brasília Legal Altamira Tucuruí Capim Rosária Parnaíba
PARÁ Itapecuru-Mirim Brejo Camocim
Itaituba Marabá Tocantins Turiaçu Viana Piripiri Granja Fortaleza (Ceará)
Caxias Caucaia
São João
do Araguaia MARANHÃO Barra do Teresina Sobral Rocas
Imperatriz Corda Codó União Maranguape Baturité Aracati
Grajaú Campo Maior Quixadá Macau
Sa. dos Carajás Pôrto Franco Colinas Amarante Oeiras Crateús CEARÁ Russas Areia Branca
Conceição do Carolina Loreto Valença do Iguatu Mossoró Ceará Mirim C. de São Roque
Araguaia Sta. Filemena Piauí Oros RIO GRANDE Natal
Araguacema Riachão Floriano Crato DO NORTE Caicó
Pedro Afonso Uruçuí PIAUÍ Juàzeiro Cajazeiras PARAÍBA Canguaretama
Paranaguá São João do Norte Cabedelo
Porto Nacional do Piauí Paulistana Cedro Campina Grande João Pessoa (Paraíba)
BRAZIL Natividade Barra Petrolina Caruaru RECIFE (Pernambuco)
Dois Irmãos Casa Nova PERNAMBUCO Garanhuns
GOIÁS Xique-Xique Juàzeiro Paulo Afonso Palmares Barreiros
Santa Isabel Remanso Senhor do Pal dos Indios Maceió
Bonfim ALAGOAS Penedo
Campo Queimadas SERGIPE
Niquelândia Formosa Barra Jacobina Itapicuru Capela Aracajú
Mundo Serrinha São Cristóvão Estância
Barreiras Novo Feira de Alagoinhas
Brasília BAHIA Itaberaba Santana
DIST. FED. Paratinga Amargosa Santo Amaro
Anápolis Bom Jesus Serra Sincorá Salvador (Bahia)
Goiânia São Francisco da Lapa Ituaçu Valença B. de Todos os Santos
Planalto do Montes Itabuna Jequié Ubaitaba Ilhéus
Mato Grosso Claros Vitória da Itacaré
GROSSO Januária Conquista Canavieiras
Monte Azul Belmonte
DO SUL Diamantina Teófilo Otoni Porto Seguro
Gov. Valadares Prado Caravelas
Campo Grande Araguari MINAS GERAIS Nanuque Mucuri Abrolhos
Uberlândia Diamantina Conceição da Barra
Aquidauana Uberaba Belo Horizonte Vitória
SÃO Juiz de Fora Campos
PAULO Petrópolis
Marília Bauru Campinas RIO DE JANEIRO Niterói
Botucatu Piracicaba

Fernando de Noronha
(Braz.)

Trindade
(Braz.)

6059

COPYRIGHT. GEORGE PHILIP & SON. LTD.

1:16 000 000

100 50 0 100 200 300 miles
100 0 100 200 300 400 km

MATO GROSSO DO SUL

PARAGUAY

PARANÁ

Asunción

Villarrica

Curitiba
Paranaguá
São Francisco do Sul

SANTA CATARINA

SÃO PAULO
Sorocaba
Santos
RIO DE JANEIRO
Mogi das Cruzes

Londrina
Maringá
Ponta Grossa

Antofagasta

San Miguel de Tucumán

Resistencia
Corrientes
Posadas
Encarnación

Santiago del Estero

Catamarca

RIO GRANDE DO SUL
Passo Fundo
Caxias do Sul
Florianópolis
Tubarão
Criciúma

La Serena
Coquimbo
Ovalle

Córdoba
Santa Fe
Paraná
Rosario

Concordia
Paysandú
URUGUAY
Rio Grande
Pelotas
Pôrto Alegre

San Juan

Mendoza
Viña del Mar
Valparaíso
SANTIAGO
Rancagua

Río Cuarto
Venado Tuerto

BUENOS AIRES
Avellaneda
MONTEVIDEO
Maldonado

Talca
Linares
Cauquenes
Parral

Santa Rosa

Mar del Plata

Talcahuano
Concepción
Chillán
Los Angeles
Victoria
Temuco
Valdivia

Neuquén
Bahía Blanca
Necochea

Osorno
Puerto Montt
Ancud

I. de Chiloé

Carlos de Bariloche

Carmen de Patagones
Viedma

Golfo San Matías
Península Valdés
Golfo Nuevo
Trelew
Rawson

Archipiélago de los Chonos

5830

Comodoro Rivadavia
Golfo San Jorge

I. Wellington

Bahía Grande

FALKLAND ISLANDS
(ISLAS MALVINAS) (Br.)
West Falkland
East Falkland
Stanley
Darwin

Río Gallegos

Estrecho de Magallanes
(Magellan's Str.)
Punta Arenas
Tierra del Fuego

South Georgia
(Br.)

Cabo de Hornos (C. Horn)

SOUTH ATLANTIC OCEAN

Peru — Chile Trench

Tropic of Capricorn

Projection: Sanson-Flamsteed's Sinusoidal

West from Greenwich

ABBREVIATIONS

Afghan. – Afghanistan	B. – Bay, Bight (Baie, Bahia, Baia)	Des. – Desert	Gt. – Great	Mor. – Morocco	Pen. – Peninsula	S. – Sea, South	Terr. – Territory
Afr. – Africa	Belg. – Belgium	Dist. – District	Hung. – Hungary	Moz. – Mozambique	Phil. – Philippines	S. Afr. – Rep. of South	Turk. – Turkey

The bold figure indicates the map page. The latitudes and longitudes are intended primarily as a guide to finding the places on the map and in some cases are only approximate.

Aac   **Ciu**

38 Ciudad Obregón, Mexico 27 28N 109 59W
13 Ciudad Real, Spain 38 59N 3 55W
38 Ciudad Victoria, Mex. 23 41N 99 9W
9 Clare, Co., Ireland 52 52N 8 35W
9 Claremorris, Ireland 53 45N 9 0W
27 Clermont, Australia 22 46S 147 38E
12 Clermont Ferrand, France 45 46N 3 4E
37 Cleveland, U.S.A. 41 28N 81 43W
6 Cleveland, Co., England 54 35N 1 20W
27 Cloncurry, Australia 20 40S 140 28E
9 Clones, Ireland 54 10N 7 13W
11 Cluj, Rumania 46 47N 23 38E
6 Clwyd, Co., Wales 53 10N 3 30W
8 Clyde, Firth of, Scotland 55 20N 5 0W
8 Clyde, R., Scotland 55 46N 3 58W
8 Clydebank, Scotland 55 54N 4 25W
36 Coast Ra., N. America 40 0N 124 0W
8 Coatbridge, Scotland 55 52N 4 2W
38 Coatzacoalcos, Mexico 18 7N 94 35W
35 Cobalt, Canada 47 25N 79 42W
9 Cobh, Ireland 51 50N 8 18W
40 Cochabamba, Bolivia 17 15S 66 20W
35 Cochrane, Canada 49 0N 81 0W
3 Cocos Is., Indian Oc. 12 12S 96 54E
22 Coimbatore, India 11 2N 76 59E
13 Coimbra, Portugal 40 15N 8 27W
7 Colchester, England 51 54N
9 Coleraine, N. Ireland 55 8N 6 40E
38 Colima, Mexico 19 10N 103 40W
8 Coll, I., Scotland 56 40N 6 3W
9 Collooney, Ireland 54 11N 8 28W
10 Cologne=Köln, W.Ger. 50 56N 8 58E
40 Colombia, St., S. America 3 45N 73 0W
22 Colombo, Sri Lanka 6 56N 79 58E
38 Colon, Panama 9 20N 80 0W
8 Colonsay, I., Scotland 56 4N 6 12W
36 Colorado, R., U.S.A. 33 30N 114 30W
36 Colorado Springs, U.S.A. 38 50N 104 50W
37 Columbia, U.S.A. 34 0N 81 0W
36 Columbia, R., U.S.A. 51 50N 118 0W
37 Columbus, Ga., U.S.A. 32 30N 84 58W
37 Columbus, Ohio, U.S.A. 39 57N 83 1W
6 Colwyn Bay, Wales 53 17N 3 44W
14 Como, Italy 45 48N 9 5E
30 Conakry, Guinea 9 29N 13 49W
42 Concepción, Chile 36 50S 73 0W
42 Concepción, Paraguay 23 30S 57 20W
42 Concordia, Argentina 31 20S 58 2W
32 Congo, R., Africa 2 0N 23 0E
32 Congo, st., Africa 2 0S 16 0E
11 Constanţa, Rumania 44 14N 28 38E
30 Constantine, Algeria 36 25N 6 30E
28 Cook Is., Pacific Oc. 22 0S 157 0W
28 Cook, Mt., N.Z. 43 36S 170 9E
28 Cook Str., N.Z. 41 15S 174 29E
27 Cooktown, Australia 15 30S 145 16E
26 Coolgardie, Australia 30 55S 121 8E
17 Copenhagen = København
27 Coarl Sea Is., Terr., 20 0S 155 0E
42 Córdoba, Argentina 31 20S 64 10W
13 Córdoba, Spain 37 50N 4 50W
15 Corfu = Kérkira, I.
9 Cork, & Co., Ireland 51 54N 8 30W
35 Corner Brook, Canada 49 0N 58 0W
7 Cornwall, Co., England 50 26N 4 40W
36 Corpus Christi, U.S.A. 27 50N 97 28W
42 Corrientes, Argentina 27 30S 58 45W
12 Corsica, I. Mediterranean Sea 42 0N 9 0E
14 Cosenza, Italy 39 17N 16 14E
39 Costa Rica st., Central America 10 0N 84 0W
30 Cotonou, Benin 6 20N 2 25E
7 Cotswold Hills, England 51 42N 2 10W
7 Coventry, England 52 25N 1 31W
27 Cowra, Australia 33 49S 148 42E
11 Craiova, Rumania 44 21N 23 48E
14 Cremona, Italy 45 8N 10 2E
15 Crete = Kriti, I. 35 20N 25 0E
6 Crewe, England 53 6N 2 28W
39 Cuba, st., W. Indies 22 0N 79 0W
40 Cúcuta, Colombia 8 0N 72 30W
40 Cuenca, Ecuador 2 50S 79 9W
13 Cuenca, Spain 45 0N 2 10W
41 Cuiabá, Brazil 15 30S 56 0W
38 Culiacan, Mexico 24 50N 107 40W
6 Cumbria, Co., England 54 30N 3 0W
6 Cumbrian, Mts., Eng. 54 30N 3 0W
27 Cunnamulla, Australia 28 2S 145 38E
40 Curaçao, Neth. W. Indies 12 10N 69 0W
40 Curaray, R., Peru 1 30S 75 30W
42 Curitiba, Brazil 25 20S 49 10W
21 Cyprus, st., Medit. Sea 35 0N 33 0E
10 Czechoslovakia, st. Europe 49 0N 17 0E
11 Czestochowa, Poland 50 49N 19 7E

D

23 Da Nang, Vietnam 16 10N 108 7E
* 22 Dacca, Bangladesh 23 43N 90 26E
30 Dahomey = Benin
30 Dakar, Senegal 14 34N 17 29W
27 Dalby, Australia 27 10S 151 17E
37 Dallas, U.S.A. 32 50N 96 50W
21 Damascus = Dimashq
26 Dampier, Australia 20 40S 116 30E
28 Dannevirke, N.Z. 40 12S 176 8E
11 Danube, R., Europe 45 0N 28 20E
32 Dar-es-Salaam, Tanzania 6 50S 39 12E
28 Dargaville, N.Z. 35 57S 173 52E
40 Darien, G. del, Colombia 9 0N 77 0W
27 Darling, R., Austral. 31 0S 144 30E
26 Darling Ra., Australia 32 30S 116 0E
6 Darlington, England 54 33N 1 33W
7 Dartmoor, England 50 36N 4 0W
35 Dartmouth, Canada 44 40N 63 30W
26 Darwin, Austral. 12 20S 130 50E
18 Daugavpils, U.S.S.R. 55 53N 26 32E
34 Dauphin, Canada 51 15N 100 5W
23 Davao, Philippines 7 0N 125 40E
39 David, Panama 8 30N 82 30W
35 Davis Str., N. America 66 30N 59 0W
34 Dawson, Canada 64 10N 139 30W

* *Now known as Dhaka*

34 Dawson Creek, Can. 55 45N 120 15W
37 Dayton, U.S.A. 39 45N 84 10W
11 Debrecen, Hungary 47 33N 21 42E
8 Dee, R., Scotland 57 4N 3 7W
22 Delhi, India 28 38N 77 17E
17 Denmark, st., Europe 55 30N 9 0E
2 Denmark Str., Atlantic Oc. 66 0N 30 0W
36 Denver, U.S.A. 39 48N 105 0W
26 Derby, Australia 17 18S 123 40E
6 Derby & Co., England 52 55N 1 28W
37 Des Moines, U.S.A. 41 29N 93 40W
37 Detroit, U.S.A. 42 20N 83 5W
7 Devon, Co., England 50 45N 3 45W
28 Devonport, N.Z. 36 49S 174 49E
6 Dewsbury, England 53 42N 1 38W
* 33 Diego-Suarez, Madagascar 12 25S 49 20E
12 Dieppe, France 49 54N 1 4E
12 Dijon, France 47 20N 5 0E
21 Dimashq (Damascus) Syria 33 30N 36 18E
8 Dingwall, Scotland 57 36N 4 26W
** 23 Djakarta, Indonesia 6 9S 106 49E
29 Djibouti, st., Africa 11 30N 43 3E
18 Dnepropetrovsk, U.S.S.R. 48 30N 35 0E
39 Dominica, I., Winward Is. 15 20N 61 20W
39 Dominican Republic, st. W. Indies 19 0N 70 30W
8 Don, R., Scotland 57 14N 2 15W
6 Doncaster, England 53 31N 1 9W
9 Donegal & Co., Ireland 54 39N 8 8W
9 Donegal, B., Ireland 54 30N 8 35W
18 Donetsk, U.S.S.R. 48 7N 37 50E
7 Dorset, Co., England 50 48N 2 25W
10 Dortmund, W. Germany 51 32N 7 28E
12 Douai, France 50 21N 3 4E
32 Douala, Cameroon 4 0N 9 45E
6 Douglas, I. of Man 54 9N 4 29W
13 Douro, R., Portugal 41 1N 8 16W
7 Dover, England 51 7N 1 19E
33 Drakensberg, Mts., S. Africa 31 0S 25 0E
17 Drammen, Norway 59 42N 10 12E
15 Drava, R., Yugoslavia 45 50N 18 0W
10 Dresden, E. Germany 51 2N 13 45E
15 Drina, R., Yugoslavia 44 30N 19 10E
9 Drogheda, Ireland 53 45N 6 20W
34 Drumheller, Canada 51 25N 112 40W
27 Dubbo, Australia 32 11S 148 35E
9 Dublin & Co., Ireland 53 20N 6 18W
15 Dubrovnik, Y-slav. 42 39N 18 6E
10 Duisburg, W. Germany 51 27N 6 42E
37 Duluth, U.S.A. 46 48N 92 10W
8 Dumbarton, Scotland 55 58N 4 35W
8 Dumfries, Scotland 55 12N 3 30W
8 Dumfries & Galloway, Co., Scot. 55 10N 3 50W
9 Dun Laoghaire, Ierland 53 17N 6 9W
9 Dundalk, Ireland 53 55N 6 45W
8 Dundee, Scotland 56 29N 3 0W
28 Dunedin, N.Z. 45 50S 170 33E
8 Dunfermline, Scotland 56 5N 3 28W
9 Dungannon, N. Ireland 54 30N 6 47W
9 Dungarvan, Ireland 52 6N 7 40W
12 Dunkerque, France 51 2N 2 20E
8 Dunnet Hd., Scotland 58 38N 3 22W
38 Durango, U.S.A. 37 10N 107 50W
33 Durban, S. Africa 29 49S 31 1E
6 Durham, Co., England 54 42N 1 45W
18 Dushanbe, U.S.S.R. 38 50N 68 50E
10 Düsseldorf, W.Ger. 51 15N 6 46E
7 Dyfed, Co., Wales 52 0N 4 0W
18 Dzerzhinsk, U.S.S.R. 56 15N 43 15E
25 Dzungaria, China 44 10N 88 0E

E

25 East China Sea, Asia 27 0N 125 0E
33 East London, S. Africa 33 0S 27 55E
7 East Sussex, Co., England 51 0N 0 30E
7 Eastbourne, England 50 46N 0 18E
22 Eastern Ghats, India 15 0N 80 0E
13 Ebro, R., Spain 41 49N 1 5W
40 Ecuador, St., S. America 22 0S 79 0W
8 Edinburgh, Scotland 55 57N 3 12W
34 Edmonton, Canada 53 30N 113 30W
35 Edmundston, Canada 47 23N 68 20W
31 Egypt, st., N. Africa 25 0N 30 0E
10 Eindhoven, Netherlands 51 26N 5 30E
31 El Faiyûm, Egypt 29 19N 30 50E
13 El Ferrol, Spain 43 29N 3 14W
31 El Gîza, Egypt 30 0N 31 10E
31 El Iskandarîya, (Alexandria) Egypt 31 0N 30 0E
31 El Khartûm, Sudan 15 31N 32 35E
31 El Marsûra, Egypt 31 0N 31 19E
31 El Minyâ, Egypt 28 7N 30 33E
31 El Obeid, Sudan 13 8N 30 10E
36 El Paso, U.S.A. 31 50N 106 30W
31 El Qâhira (Cairo) Egypt 30 1N 31 14E
31 El Suweis (Suez) Egypt 29 58N 32 31E
14 Elba, I., Italy 42 48N 10 15E
10 Elbe, R. Germany 53 15N 10 7E
18 Elbrus, Mt., U.S.S.R. 43 30N 42 30E
21 Elburz Mts., Iran 36 0N 52 0E
13 Elche, Spain 38 15N 0 42W
8 Elgin, Scotland 57 39N 3 20W
2 Ellesmere I., Canada 79 30N 80 0W
3 Ellice Is. (Tuvalu), Pacific Oc. 8 0S 176 0E
27 Emerald, Australia 23 30S 148 11E
38 Empalme, Mexico 28 1N 110 49W
3 Enderby Land, Antarctica 66 0S 53 0E
18 Engels, U.S.S.R. 51 28N 46 6E
6 England, U.K. 50 to 55 45N 1 40E to 5 40W
7 English Chan., Europe 50 0N 2 0W
9 Ennis, Ireland 52 51N 8 59W
9 Enniskillen, N. Ireland 52 30N 6 35W
32 Entebbe, Uganda 0 3N 32 30E
30 Enugu, Nigeria 6 30N 7 30E
32 Equatorial Guinea, st., Africa 2 0N 10 E
37 Erie, U.S.A. 42 7N 80 2W
37 Erie, L., N. America 42 30N 82 0W
31 Eritrea, Reg., Ethiopia 14 0N 41 0E

* *Renamed Antseranana*
** *Also known as Jakarta*

9 Erne, L., N. Ireland 54 14N 7 30W
21 Erzurum, Turkey 39 57N 41 15E
17 Esbjerg, Denmark 55 29N 8 29E
21 Esfahan, Iran 32 43N 51 33E
17 Eskilstuna, Sweden 59 22N 16 32E
26 Esperance, Australia 33 45S 121 55E
40 Essequibo, R., Guyana 5 45N 58 50W
10 Essen, W. Germany 51 28N 6 59E
7 Essex, Co., England 51 48N 0 30E
31 Ethiopia, st., Africa 8 0N 40 0E
14 Etna, Mt., Italy 37 45N 15 0E
36 Eugene, U.S.A. 44 0N 123 8W
21 Euphrates, R., Iraq 33 30N 43 0E
37 Evansville, U.S.A. 38 0N 87 35W
22 Everest, Mt., Nepal 28 5N 86 58E
15 Evvoia, I., Greece 38 30N 24 0E
7 Exeter, England 50 43N 3 31W
27 Eyre, L., Australia 29 0S 137 20E
26 Eyre Pen., Australia 33 30S 137 17E

F

17 Fagersta, Sweden 60 1N 15 46E
34 Fairbanks, Alaska 64 59N 147 40W
8 Falkirk, Scotland 56 0N 3 47W
42 Falkland Islands, Atlantic Oc. 51 30S 58 30W
2 Falkland Islands Dependencies, Southern Oc. 55 0S 45 0W
17 Falun, Sweden 60 32N 15 39E
7 Fareham, England 50 52N 1 11W
37 Fargo, U.S.A. 47 0N 97 0W
2 Faroe Is., N. Atlantic Oc. 62 0N 7 0W
28 Fielding, N.Z. 40 13S 175 35E
7 Felixtowe, England 51 58N 1 22W
14 Ferrard, Italy 44 50N 11 26E
30 Fés, Morocco 34 5N 4 54W
8 Fife, Co., Scotland 56 13N 3 2W
28 Fiji, Is., Pacific Ocean 17 20S 179 0E
8 Findhorn, R., Scotland 57 30N 3 45W
13 Finisterre, C., Spain 42 50N 9 19W
16 Finland, st., Europe 70 0N 27 0E
14 Firenze, Italy 43 47N 11 15E
7 Fishguard, Wales 51 59N 4 59W
6 Flamborough Hd., Eng. 54 8N 0 4W
10 Flensburg, Germany 54 46N 9 28E
27 Flinders Ra., Australia 31 30S 138 30E
37 Flint, U.S.A. 43 0N 83 40W
23 Flores Sea, Indonesia 6 30S 124 0E
14 Florence = Firenze
42 Florianópolis, Brazil 27 30S 48 30W
37 Florida Str., U.S.A. 25 0N 80 0W
14 Fóggia, Italy 41 28N 15 31E
7 Folkestone, England 51 5N 1 11E
12 Fontainbleau, France 48 24N 2 40E
25 Foochow, China 26 9N 119 25E
25 Formosa = Taiwan
4 Føroyar, Is., Atlantic Oc. 62 0N 7 0W
37 Fort Smith, U.S.A. 35 25N 94 25W
37 Fort Wayne, U.S.A. 41 5N 85 10W
8 Fort William, Scotland 56 48N 5 8W
36 Fort Worth, U.S.A. 32 45N 97 25W
34 Fort Yukon, Alaska 66 35N 145 12W
39 Fort-de-France, Martinique 14 36N 61 2W
41 Fortaleza, Brazil 3 35S 38 35W
8 Forth, Firth of, Scotland 56 5N 2 55W
12 France, st., Europe 47 0N 3 0E
10 Frankfurt, W. Germany 50 7N 8 40E
34 Fraser, R., Canada 53 30N 120 40W
8 Fraserburgh, Scotland 57 41N 2 0W
35 Fredericton, Canada 45 57N 66 40W
17 Frederikshavn, Den. 57 28N 10 31E
17 Fredrikstad, Norway 59 13N 10 57E
39 Freeport, Bahamas 42 18N 89 40W
30 Freetown, Sierra Leone 8 30N 13 10W
10 Freiburg, Germany 48 0N 7 52E
26 Fremantle, Australia 32 1S 115 47E
41 French Guiana, S. America 4 0N 53 0W
38 Fresnillo, Mexico 23 10N 103 0W
36 Fresno, U.S.A. 36 47N 119 50W
18 Frunze, U.S.S.R. 42 40N 74 50E
24 Fukuoka, Japan 33 30N 130 30E
24 Funabashi, Japan 33 45N 140 0E
27 Furneaux Group, Is., Tasmania 40 10S 147 56E
25 Fushun, China 41 55N 123 55E
17 Fyn, I., Denmark 55 18N 10 20E
8 Fyne, L., Denmark 55 20N 10 30E

G

32 Gabon, st., Africa 2 0S 12 0E
15 Gabrovo, Bulgaria 42 52N 25 27E
2 Galapagos Is., Pacific Oc. 0 0 89 0W
11 Galaţi, Rumania 45 27N 28 2E
16 Gällivare, Sweden 67 7N 20 32E
8 Galloway, Mull of, Scot. 54 38N 4 50W
37 Galveston, U.S.A. 29 15N 94 48W
9 Galway & Co., Ireland 53 16N 9 4W
9 Galway, B., Ireland 53 10N 9 20W
30 Gambia, st., W. Africa 13 25N 16 0W
22 Ganga, R., India 25 0N 88 0E
22 Ganges, R. = Ganga R.
14 Garda, L. di, Italy 45 40N 10 40E
12 Garonne, R., France 44 45N 0 32W
35 Gaspé Pen., Canada 48 45N 65 40W
6 Gateshead, England 54 57N 1 37W
17 Gävle, Sweden 60 41N 17 13E
31 Gaza, Egypt 31 30N 34 28E
11 Gdańsk, Poland 54 22N 18 40E
11 Gdyñia, Poland 54 35N 18 33E
27 Geelong, Australia 38 2S 144 20E
10 Genève, Switzerland 46 12N 6 9E
14 Génova (Genoa) Italy 44 24N 8 56E
10 Gent, Belgium 51 2N 3 37E
40 Georgetown, Guyana 6 50N 58 12W
26 Geraldton, Australia 28 48S 114 32E
10 Germany, East, st. Europe 52 0N 12 0E
10 Germany, West, st., Europe 52 0N 9 0E
33 Germiston, S. Africa 26 11S 28 10E
13 Gerona, Spain 41 58N 2 46E
30 Ghana, st., W. Africa 6 0N 1 0W
9 Giant's Causeway, N. Ireland 55 15N 6 30W
13 Gibraltar, Europe 36 7N 5 22W
26 Gibson Desert, Australia 24 0S 125 0E
24 Gifu, Japan 35 30N 136 45E

13 Gijón, Spain 43 32N 5 42W
* 3 Gilbert Is., Pacific Oc. 1 0S 176 0E
7 Gillingham, England 51 23N 0 34E
8 Girvan, Scotland 55 15N 4 50W
28 Gisborne, N.Z. 38 39S 178 5E
17 Gjøvik, Norway 60 47N 10 43E
35 Glace Bay, Canada 46 11N 59 58W
27 Gladstone, Australia 23 52S 151 16E
17 Glamå, R., Norway 60 30N 12 8E
8 Glasgow, Scotland 55 52N 4 14W
27 Glen Innes, Australia 29 40S 151 39E
36 Glendale, U.S.A. 34 7N 118 18W
7 Gloucester & Co., England 51 52N 2 15W
22 Godavari, R., India 19 5N 79 0E
41 Goiânia, Brazil 16 35S 49 20W
18 Gomel, U.S.S.R. 52 28N 31 0E
38 Gómez Palacio, Mexico 25 40N 104 40W
33 Good Hope, C. of, S. Africa 34 24S 18 30E
28 Gore, N.Z. 46 5S 168 58E
18 Gorkiy, U.S.S.R. 57 20N 44 0E
7 Gosport, England 50 48N 1 8W
17 Göteborg, Sweden 57 43N 11 59E
17 Gotland, I., Swdeen 58 15N 18 30E
27 Goulburn, Australia 32 22S 149 31E
41 Governador Valadares, Brazil 18 15S 41 57W
14 Gozo, I., Malta 36 0N 14 13E
27 Grafton, Australia 29 35S 152 0E
2 Graham Land, Antacrtica 67 0S 65 0W
33 Grahamstown, S. Africa 33 19S 26 31E
8 Grampian, Co., Scot. 57 30N 2 40W
8 Grampian Highlands, Scotland 56 50N 4 0W
39 Granada, Nicaragua 11 58N 86 0W
13 Granada, Spain 37 10N 3 35W
36 Grand Canyon, U.S.A. 36 20N 113 30W
37 Grand Forks, U.S.A. 48 0N 97 3W
37 Grand Rapids, U.S.A. 42 57N 85 40W
34 Grande Prairie, Can. 55 15N 118 50W
10 Graz, Austria 47 4N 15 27E
39 Great Abaco, I. Bahamas 26 30N 77 20W
26 Great Australian Bight, Australia 33 0S 130 0E
27 Great Barrier Reef, Australia 19 0S 149 0E
34 Great Bear L., Canada 65 0N 120 0W
27 Great Divide, Mts., Australia 23 0S 146 0E
36 Great Falls, U.S.A. 47 29N 111 19W
36 Great Salt L. U.S.A. 41 0N 112 30W
26 Great Sandy Desert, Australia 21 0S 124 0E
34 Great Slave L., Can. 61 30N 114 20W
26 Great Victoria Desert, Australia 29 30S 126 30E
6 Great Yarmouth, Eng. 52 40N 1 45E
39 Greater Antilles, W. Indies 17 40N 74 0W
15 Greece, St. Europe 40 0N 23 0E
37 Green Bay, U.S.A. 44 30N 88 0W
35 Greenland, N. America 66 0N 45 0W
8 Greenock, Scotland 55 57N 4 46W
37 Greensboro, U.S.A. 36 5N 79 47W
39 Grenada I., W. Indies 12 10N 61 40W
12 Grenoble, France 45 12N 5 42E
28 Greymouth, N.Z. 42 29S 171 13E
27 Griffith, Australia 34 14S 145 46E
6 Grimsby, England 53 35N 0 5W
18 Grodno, U.S.S.R. 53 42N 23 52E
10 Groningen, Netherlands 53 15N 6 35E
18 Groznyy, U.S.S.R. 43 20N 45 45E
38 Guadalajara, Mexico 20 40N 103 20W
13 Guadalquiver, R., Spain 38 0N 4 0W
39 Guadeloupe, I., Fr. W. Indies 16 20N 61 40W
13 Guadiana, R., Spain 37 55N 7 39W
13 Guadix, Spain 37 18N 3 11W
39 Guanabacoa, Cuba 23 8N 82 18W
39 Guantánamo, Cuba 20 10N 75 20W
42 Guarapuava, Brazil 25 20S 51 30W
38 Guatemala, st. Central America 15 40N 90 30W
38 Guatemala, Guatemala, 14 40N 90 30
40 Guaviare, R., Colombia 3 30N 71 0W
40 Guayaquil, Ecuador 2 15N 79 52W
38 Guaymas, Mexico 27 50N 111 0W
7 Guernsey, I., Brit. Isles 49 30N 2 35W
7 Guildford, England 51 14N 0 34W
30 Guinea, st., W. Africa 10 20N 10 0W
29 Guinea, G. of, W. Africa 3 0N 2 30E
30 Guinea-Bissau, st., W. Africa 12 0N 15 0W
22 Gujranwala, Pakistan 32 10N 74 12E
18 Guryev, U.S.S.R. 47 5N 52 0E
40 Guyana, St., S. America 5 0N 59 0W
22 Gwalior, India 26 12N 78 10E
** 33 Gwelo, Zimbabwe 19 28S 29 45E
7 Gwent, Co., Wales 51 40N 3 0W
6 Gwynedd, Co., Wales 53 0N 4 0N
27 Gympie, Australia 26 11S 152 38E

H

10 Haarlem, Netherlands 52 23N 4 39E
24 Hachiōji, Japan 35 30N 139 30E
21 Haifa, Israel 32 48N 35 0E
39 Haiti, st., W. Indies 19 6N 72 30W
24 Hakodate, Japan 41 45N 140 44E
21 Halab (Aleppo) Syria 36 12N 37 13E
35 Halifax, Canada 44 38N 63 35W
6 Halifax, England 53 43N 1 51W
10 Halle, E. Germany 51 29N 12 0E
23 Halmahera, I., Indonesia 0 40N 128 0E
17 Halmstad, Sweden 56 37N 12 56E
21 Hamá, Syria 35 5N 36 40E
21 Hamadan, Iran 34 52N 48 32E
17 Hamar, Norway 60 48N 11 7E
24 Hamamatsu, Japan 34 45N 137 45E
10 Hamburg W. Germany 53 32N 9 59E
17 Hämeenlinna, Finland 61 3N 24 26E
35 Hamilton, Canada 43 20N 79 50W
28 Hamilton, N.Z. 37 47S 175 19E
8 Hamilton, Scotland 55 47N 4 2W
16 Hammerfest, Norway 70 33N 23 50E

* *Now part of Kiribati*
** *Renamed Gweru*

7 Hampshire, Co., England 51 3N 1 20W
25 Hangchow, China 30 20N 120 5E
17 Hangö, Finland 59 59N 22 57E
10 Hannover, W. Germany 52 23N 9 43E
23 Hanoi, Vietnam 21 5N 105 40E
16 Haparanda, Sweden 65 52N 24 8E
25 Harbin, China 45 45N 126 41E
16 Härnösand, Sweden 62 38N 18 5E
8 Harris, Scotland 57 50N 6 55W
37 Harrisburg, U.S.A. 40 18N 76 52W
6 Harrogate, England 53 59N 1 32W
37 Hartford, U.S.A. 41 47N 72 41W
6 Hartlepool, England 54 42N 1 11W
7 Harwich, England 51 56N 1 18E
7 Hastings, England 50 51N 0 36E
28 Hastings, N.Z. 39 39S 176 52E
36 Hawaiian Is., Pacific Oc. 20 0N 155 0W
8 Hawick, Scotland 55 25N 2 48W
27 Hawker, Australia 31 59S 138 22E
35 Hearst, Canada 49 40N 83 41W
10 Heidelberg, W. Ger. 49 23N 8 41E
17 Helsingborg, Sweden 56 3N 12 42E
17 Helsingør, Denmark 56 2N 12 35E
17 Helsinki, Finland 60 15N 25 3E
25 Hengyang, China 26 58N 112 25E
21 Herat, Afghanistan 34 20N 62 7E
7 Hereford, England 52 4N 2 42W
7 Hereford & Worcester, Co., England 52 4N 2 43W
38 Hermosillo, Mexico 29 10N 111 0W
7 Hertfordshire, Co., England 51 51N 0 5W
24 Hida-Sammyaku, Japan 36 30N 137 40E
38 Hidalgo del Parral, Mexico 26 10N 104 50W
7 High Wycombe, Eng. 51 37N 0 45W
8 Highland, Co., Scotland 57 30N 5 0W
36 Hilo, Hawaiian Is. 19 42N 155 4W
22 Himalaya, Mts., Asia 29 0N 84 0E
24 Himeji, Japan 34 50N 134 40E
21 Hindu Kush, Ra., Afghan. 36 0N 71 0E
24 Hiroshima, Japan 34 30N 132 30E
39 Hispaniola, I., W. Indies 19 0N 71 0W
17 Hjørring, Denmark 57 29N 9 59E
27 Hobart, Tasmania 42 50S 147 21E
24 Hokkaido, I., Japan 43 30N 143 0E
39 Holguín, Cuba 20 50N 76 20W
6 Holyhead, Wales 53 18N 4 38W
39 Honduras, Rep. Central America 14 40N 86 30W
17 Hønefoss, Norway 60 10N 10 12E
25 Hong Kong, Br. Crown Colony, Asia 22 11N 14 14E
36 Honolulu, Hawaiian Is. 21 25N 157 55W
24 Honshu, I., Japan 36 0N 138 0E
42 Horn, C., Chile 55 50S 67 30W
17 Horsens, Denmark 55 52N 9 50E
17 Horten, Norway 59 25N 10 32E
13 Hospitalet, Spain 41 21N 2 6E
37 Houston, U.S.A. 29 50N 95 20W
7 Hove, England 50 50N 0 10W
22 Howrah, India 22 37N 88 27E
25 Hsiamen, China 24'30N 118 7E
33 Murambo, Angola 12 42S 15 54W
6 Huddersfield, England 53 38N 1 49W
35 Hudson, B., Canada 60 0N 86 0W
37 Hudson, R., U.S.A. 41 35N 74 0W
35 Hudson Str., Canada 62 0N 70 0W
23 Hue, Vietnam 16 60N 107 35E
13 Huelva, Spain 37 18N 6 57W
13 Huesca, Spain 42 8N 0 25W
27 Hughenden, Australia 20 52S 144 10E
35 Hull, Canada 45 20N 75 40W
6 Hull, England 53 45N 0 20W
6 Humber, R., England 53 42N 0 20W
6 Humberside, Co., Eng. 53 40N 0 30W
11 Hungary, Rep. Europe 47 20N 19 20E
37 Huntingdon, U.S.A. 38 20N 82 30W
35 Huron, L., N. America 45 0N 83 0W
25 Hwang-Ho, R., China 40 50N 107 30E
22 Hyderabad, India 17 10N 78 20E
22 Hyderabad, Pakistan 25 23N 68 36E

I

11 Iaşi, Rumania 47 10N 27 40E
30 Ibadan, Nigeria 7 22N 3 58E
40 Ibagué, Colombia 4 27N 73 14W
13 Ibiza, I., Spain 39 0N 1 30E
16 Iceland, Rep., Europe 65 0N 19 0W
24 Ichinomiya, Japan 35 20N 136 50E
30 Ife, Nigeria 7 30N 4 31E
23 Iloilo, Philippines, 10 45N 122 33E
25 Inchon, S. Korea 37 30N 126 30E
22 India, St., Asia 23 0N 80 0E
20 Indian Ocean 5 0S 75 0E
37 Indianapolis, U.S.A. 39 42N 86 10W
23 Indonesia, Rep., Asia 5 0S 115 0E
22 Indore, India 22 42N 75 53E
22 Indus, R., Pakistan 28 40N 70 10E
27 Ingham, Australia 18 43S 146 10E
33 Inhambane, Moz. 23 51S 35 29E
8 Inner Hebrides, Is., Scotland 58 0N 7 0W
10 Innsbruck, Austria 47 16N 11 23E
28 Invercargill, N.Z. 46 24S 168 24E
8 Inverness, Scotland 57 29N 4 12W
15 Ionian Sea, Europe 37 30N 17 30E
27 Ipswich, Australia 27 38S 152 37E
7 Ipswich, England 52 4N 1 9E
40 Iquique, Chile 20 19S 70 5W
40 Iquitos, Peru 3 45S 73 10W
15 Iráklion, Greece 35 20N 25 12E
21 Iran, st., Asia 33 0N 53 0E
21 Iraq, st., Asia 33 0N 44 0E
9 Ireland, Rep., Europe 53 0N 8 0W
23 Irian Jaya, Indonesia 4 0S 137 0E
5 Irish Sea, Europe 54 0N 5 0W
19 Irkutsk, U.S.S.R. 52 10N 104 20E
8 Islay, I., Scotland 55 46N 6 10W
31 Ismâ'ilîa, Egypt 30 47N 32 18E
21 Israel, st., Asia 32 30N 32 30E
21 Istanbul, Turkey 41 0N 29 0E
41 Itabuna, Brazil 14 48S 39 16W
14 Itlay, Rep., Europe 42 0N 13 0E
18 Ivanovo, U.S.S.R. 57 5N 41 0E
30 Ivory Coast, st., W. Africa 7 30N 5 0W

30 Iwo, Nigeria 7 39N 4 9E
† 18 Izhevsk, U.S.S.R. 56 50N 53 0E
21 Izmir, Turkey 38 25N 27 8E

J

22 Jabalpur, India 23 9N 79 58E
37 Jackson, U.S.A. 32 20N 90 10W
37 Jacksonville, U.S.A. 30 15N 81 38W
13 Jaén, Spain 37 44N 3 43W
22 Jaipur, India 20 51N 86 28E
38 Jalapa, Mexico 19 30N 96 50W
39 Jamaica, I., W. Indies 18 10N 77 30W
35 James, .B, Canada 53 30N 80 30W
22 Jamshedpur, India 22 44N 86 20E
24 Japan, st., Asia 36 0N 136 0E
24 Japan, Sea of, Asia 40 0N 135 0E
41 Jau, Brazil 22 10S 48 30W
23 Java, I., Indonesia 7 0S 110 0E
13 Jerez, Spain 36 41N 6 7W
7 Jersey, I., British Isles 49 13N 2 7W
37 Jersey City, U.S.A. 40 41N 74 8W
21 Jerusalem, Israel 31 47N 35 10E
21 Jidda, Saudi Arabia 21 29N 39 16E
41 João Pessoa, Brazil 7 10S 35 0W
22 Jodhpur, India 26 23N 73 2E
* 23 Jogjakarta, Indonesia 6 9S 106 49E
33 Johannesburg, S. Africa 26 10S 28 8E
8 John O'Groats, Scot. 58 39N 3 3W
17 Jönköping, Sweden 57 45N 14 10E
21 Jordan, st., Asia 31 0N 36 0E
17 Jotunheimen, Mts., Norway 61 30N 9 0E
41 Juàzeiro do Norte, Brazil 7 10S 39 18W
41 Juiz de Fora, Brazil 21 43S 43 19W
22 Jullundur, India 31 20N 75 40E
34 Juneau, Alaska 58 21N 134 20W
8 Jura, I., Scotland 56 0N 5 50W
12 Jura, Mts., Europe 46 35N 6 5E
40 Juruá, R., Brazil 5 20S 67 40W
16 Jyväskylä, Finland 62 12N 25 47E

K

21 Kabul, Afghanistan 34 28N 69 18E
30 Kaduna, Nigeria 10 30N 7 21E
24 Kagoshima, Japan 31 36N 130 40E
23 Kaifeng, China 34 45N 114 30E
16 Kajaani, Finland 64 17N 27 46E
33 Kalahari, Desert, Africa 24 0S 22 0E
32 Kalemie, Zaïre 5 55S 29 9E
26 Kalgoorlie, Australia 30 40S 121 22E
18 Kalinin, U.S.S.R. 56 55N 35 55E
18 Kaliningrad, U.S.S.R. 54 42N 20 32E
17 Kalmar, Sweden 56 39N 16 22E
18 Kaluga, U.S.S.R. 54 35N 36 10E
32 Kamina, Zaïre 8 45S 25 0E
34 Kamloops, Canada 50 40N 120 20W
32 Kampala, Uganda 0 20N 32 30E
32 Kananga, Zaïre 5 55S 22 18E
24 Kanazawa, Japan 36 30N 136 38E
21 Kandahar, Afghanistan 31 32N 65 30E
18 Kandalaksha, U.S.S.R. 67 9N 32 30E
22 Kandy, Sri Lanka 7 18N 80 43E
30 Kano, Nigeria 12 0N 8 30E
22 Kanpur, India 26 35N 80 20E
37 Kansas City, U.S.A. 39 0N 94 37W
25 Kaohsiung, Taiwan 22 35N 120 16E
22 Karachi, Pakistan 24 53N 67 0E
18 Karanganda, U.S.S.R. 49 50N 73 0E
22 Karakorum, Mts., India 35 20N 78 0E
21 Karbala, Iraq 32 47N 44 3E
33 Kariba, L. Zambia-Zimbabwe 16 40S 28 20E
10 Karl-Marx-Stadt, E. Germany 50 50N 12 55E
17 Karlskrona, Sweden 56 12N 15 42E
10 Karlsruhe, W. Germany 49 3N 8 23E
17 Karlstad, Sweden 59 24N 13 35E
32 Kasai, R., Zaïre 8 20S 22 0E
10 Kassel, W. Germany 51 19N 9 32E
26 Katherine, Australia 14 27S 132 20E
22 Katmandu, Nepal 27 45N 85 12E
27 Katoomba, Australia 33 30N 150 0E
11 Katowice Poland, 50 17N 19 5E
30 Katsina, Nigeria 7 10N 9 20E
17 Kattegat, Str., Denmark 56 50N 11 20E
18 Kaunas, U.S.S.R. 54 54N 23 54E
24 Kawaguchi, Japan 35 52N 138 45E
24 Kawasaki, Japan 35 40N 139 45E
28 Kawerau, N.Z. 38 7S 176 42E
18 Kazan, U.S.S.R. 55 48N 49 3E
15 Kazanlŭk, Bulgaria 42 38N 25 35E
33 Keetmanshoop, S. W. Africa 26 35S 18 8E
16 Keflavik, Iceland 64 2N 22 35W
6 Keighley, England 53 52N 1 54W
18 Kemerovo, U.S.S.R. 55 20N 85 50W
16 Kemi, Finland 65 48N 24 43E
34 Kenora, Canada 49 50N 94 35W
7 Kent, Co., England 51 12N 0 40E
32 Kenya, st., E. Africa 0 5N 37 0E
3 Kerguelen, I., Indian Oc. 48 30S 69 40E
15 Kérkira, I., Greece 39 40N 19 50E
28 Kermadec Is., Pacific Oc. 31 8S 175 16W
21 Kerman, Iarn 30 15N 57 1E
** 21 Kermanshah, Iran 34 23N 47 0E
9 Kerry, Co., Ireland 52 7N 9 35W
37 Key West, U.S.A. 24 40N 82 0W
19 Kharbarovsk, U.S.S.R. 48 20N 135 0E
18 Kharkov, U.S.S.R. 49 58N 36 20E
31 Khartoum = El Khartûm
15 Khaskovo, Bulgaria 41 56N 25 30E
18 Kherson, U.S.S.R. 46 35N 32 35E
15 Khíos, I., Greece 38 23N 29 0E
22 Khulna, Bangladesh 22 45N 89 34E
10 Kiel, W. Germany 54 16N 10 8E
15 Kikládhes, Is., Greece 37 50N 25 0E
9 Kildare, Co., Ireland 53 10N 6 50W
32 Kilimanjaro, Mt., Tanzania 3 4S 37 21E
9 Kilkenny & Co., Ireland 52 40N 7 17W
9 Killarney, Ireland 52 2N 9 30W
8 Kilmarnock, Scotland 55 36N 4 30W
33 Kimberley, S. Africa 28 43N 24 46E
27 King I., Australia 39 40S 144 0E
6 King's Lynn, England 52 45N 0 25E
35 Kingston, Canada 44 20N 76 30W
32 Kinshasa, Zaïre 4 20N 15 15E

* Renamed Yogyakarta
** Renamed Bakhtaran
† Renamed Ustinov

19 Kirensk, U.S.S.R. 57 50N 107 55E
25 Kirin, China 43 50N 126 38E
8 Kirkcaldy, Scotland 56 7N 3 10W
35 Kirkland Lake, Canada 48 15N 80 0W
21 Kirkuk, Iraq 35 30N 44 21E
8 Kirkwall, Scotland 58 59N 2 59W
18 Kirov, U.S.S.R. 58 25N 49 40E
18 Kirovogard, U.S.S.R. 48 35N 32 20E
16 Kiruna, Sweden 67 50N 20 20E
32 Kisangani, Zaïre 0 41N 25 11E
18 Kiselevsk, U.S.S.R. 54 5N 86 6E
18 Kishinev, U.S.S.R. 47 1N 28 50E
29 Kismayu, Somalia 0 20S 42 30E
24 Kitakyûshû, Japan 33 50N 130 50E
35 Kitchener, Canada 43 30N 80 30W
33 Kitwe, Zambia 12 50S 28 0E
18 Kiyev, U.S.S.R. 50 30N 30 28E
10 Klagenfurt, Austria 46 38N 14 20E
37 Knoxville, U.S.A. 35 58N 83 57W
24 Kōbe, Japan 34 45N 135 10E
17 København, (Copenhagen) Denmark 55 41N 12 34E
10 Koblenz, W. Germany 50 21N 7 36E
24 Kōchi, Japan 33 30N 133 35E
16 Kokkola, Finlnad 63 50N 23 8E
17 Kolding, Denmark 55 30N 9 29E
22 Kolhapur, India 16 43N 74 15E
10 Köln, W. Germany 50 56N 9 58E
18 Kolomna, U.S.S.R. 55 8N 38 45E
32 Kolwezi, Zaïre 10 40S 25 25E
19 Komsomolsk, U.S.S.R. 50 30N 137 0E
18 Kopeysk, U.S.S.R. 54 55N 61 31E
15 Korab, Mt., Y-slav. 41 44N 20 40E
24 Kōriyama, Japan 37 10N 140 18E
27 Kosciusko, Mt., Australia 36 27S 148 16E
11 Kosice, Czechoslovakia 48 42N 21 15E
18 Kostroma, U.S.S.R. 57 50N 41 58E
25 Kowloon, Hong Kong 22 25N 114 10E
15 Kragujevac, Yugoslavia 44 2N 20 56E
11 Krakow, Poland 50 4N 19 57E
18 Krasnodar, U.S.S.R. 45 5N 38 50E
18 Krasnovodsk, U.S.S.R. 50 0N 52 52E
19 Krasnoyarsk, U.S.S.R. 56 8N 93 0E
18 Kremenchug, U.S.S.R. 49 5N 33 25E
17 Kristiansand, Norway 58 9N 8 1E
16 Kristiansund, Norway 63 10N 7 45E
16 Kristinestad, Finland 62 16N 21 21E
15 Kriti, I., (Crete) Greece 35 15N 25 0E
18 Krivoy Rog, U.S.S.R. 47 51N 33 20E
33 Krugersdorp, S. Africa 26 5S 27 46E
23 Krung Thep (Bangkok) Thailand 13 45N 100 31E
23 Kuala Lumpur, Malaysia 3 9N 101 41E
24 Kumamoto, Japan 32 45N 130 45E
30 Kumasi, Ghana 6 41N 1 38W
32 Kumba, Cameroon 4 36N 9 24E
25 Kunlun Shan, Asia 36 0N 86 30E
25 Kunming, China 25 0N 102 45E
26 Kununurra, Australia 15 40S 128 39E
16 Kuopio, Finland 62 53N 27 35E
24 Kurashiki, Japan 34 40N 133 50E
24 Kure, Japan 33 15N 133 15E
18 Kurgan, U.S.S.R. 55 30N 65 0E
18 Kursk, U.S.S.R. 51 42N 36 11E
18 Kustanai, U.S.S.R. 53 20N 63 45E
21 Kuwait = Al Kuwayt
21 Kuwait, st., Asia 29 30N 47 30E
18 Kuybyshev, U.S.S.R. 53 20N 57 0E
25 Kwangchow, China 23 10N 113 10E
25 Kweiyang, China 26 30N 106 35E
8 Kyle of Lochalsh, Scotland 57 17N 5 43 W
24 Kyushu, I., Japan 32 30N 131 0E

L

39 La Ceiba, Honduras 15 40N 86 50W
13 La Coruña, Spain 43 20N 8 25W
39 La Habana, Cuba 23 8N 82 22W
13 La Linea de la Concepción, Spain 36 15N 5 23W
40 La Paz, Bolivia 16 20S 68 10W
38 La Paz, Mexico 24 10N 110 20W
38 La Piedad, Mexico 20 20N 102 1W
42 La Plata, Argentina 35 0S 57 55W
12 La Rochelle, France 46 10N 1 9W
39 La Romana, Dominican Rep. 18 27N 68 57W
42 La Serena, Chile 29 55S 71 10W
14 La Spézia, Italy 44 8N 9 48E
35 Labrador, Reg., Canada 53 20N 61 0W
23 Labuan, I. Malaysia 5 15N 115 38W
22 Laccadive Is., Indian Oc. 10 0N 72 30E
9 Lagan, R., N. Ireland 54 35N 5 55W
30 Lagos, Nigeria 6 25N 3 27E
13 Lagos, Portugal 37 5N 8 41W
22 Lahore, Pakistan 31 32N 74 22E
17 Lahti, Finland 60 59N 25 45E
37 Lakewood, U.S.A. 41 28N 81 50W
6 Lancashire, Co., England 53 5N 2 30W
6 Lancaster, England 54 3N 2 48W
25 Lanchow, China 36 0N 103 50E
7 Land's End, England 50 4N 5 43W
12 Langrse, France 47 52N 5 20E
37 Lansing, U.S.A. 42 47N 84 32W
9 Laois, Co., Ireland 53 0N 7 20W
23 Laos, st., Asia 17 45N 105 0E
19 Lapter Sea, '.S.S.R. 76 0N 125 0E
14 L'Aquila, Italy 42 21N 13 24E
36 Laredo, U.S.A. 27 34N 99 29W
15 Lárisa, Greece 39 38N 22 28E
17 Larvik, Norway 59 4N 10 0E
30 Las Palmas, Canary Is. 28 10N 15 28W
36 Las Vegas, U.S.A. 36 10N 115 5W
27 Launceston, Australia 41 24S 147 8E
10 Lausanne, Switzerland 46 32N 6 38E
12 Le Havre, France 49 30N 0 5E
12 Le Mans, France 48 0N 0 12E
7 Leamington, England 52 18N 1 32W
21 Lebanon, st., Asia 34 0N 36 0E
15 Lecce, Italy 40 20N 18 10E
6 Leeds, England 53 48N 1 34W
39 Leeward Is., W. Indies 16 30N 63 30W
14 Leghorn = Livorno
7 Leicester & Co., England 52 39N 1 9W
10 Leipzig, E. Germany 51 20N 12 23E
8 Leith, Scotland 55 55N 3 11W
9 Leitrim, Co., Ireland 54 8N 8 0W
10 Léman, L. Switzerland 46 26N 6 30E
18 Leningrad, U.S.S.R. 59 55N 30 20E
18 Leninsk Kuznetskiy U.S.S.R. 55 10N 86 10E
38 León, Mexico 21 7N 101 30W
39 León, Nicaragua 12 20N 86 51W
13 León, Spain 42 38N 5 34W
13 Lérida, Spain 41 37N 0 39E
8 Lerwick, Scotland 60 10N 1 10W
33 Lesotho, st., Africa 29 40S 28 0E
15 Lésvos, I., Greece 26 0N 39 15E
34 Lethbridge, Canada 49 45N 112 45W
28 Levin, N.Z. 40 37S 175 18E
21 Levkösia, Cyprus 35 10N 33 25E
8 Lewis, I., Scotland 58 10N 6 40W
37 Lexington, U.S.A. 38 6N 84 30W
25 Lhasa, Tibet, China 29 40N 91 10E
30 Liberia, st., W. Africa 6 30N 9 30W
32 Libreville, Gabon 0 25N 9 26E
31 Libya, st., N. Africa 28 30N 17 30E
10 Liechtenstein, st., Europe 47 8N 9 35E
9 Liffey, R., Ireland 53 21N 6 20W
9 Lifford, Ireland 54 50N 7 30W
14 Ligurian Sea, Europe 43 20N 9 0E
32 Likasi, Zaïre 10 55S 26 48E
12 Lille, France 50 38N 3 3E
17 Lillehammer, Norway 61 8N 10 30E
33 Lilongwe, Malawi 14 0S 33 48E
40 Lima, Peru 12 0S 77 0W
37 Lima, U.S.A. 40 42N 84 5W
9 Limerick & Co., Ireland 52 40N 8 38W
15 Límnos, I., Greece 39 50N 25 15E
12 Limoges, France 45 50N 1 15E
39 Limón, Costa Rica 10 0N 83 2W
33 Limpopo, R. Africa 24 15S 32 45E
13 Linares, Spain 38 10N 3 40W
6 Lincoln & Co., England 53 11N 0 20W
37 Lincoln, U.S.A. 40 50N 96 42W
17 Linköping, Sweden 58 28N 15 36E
8 Linnhe, L., Scotland 56 36N 5 25W
10 Linz, Austria 48 18N 14 18E
14 Lípari, Is., Italy 38 40N 15 0E
18 Lipetsk, U.S.S.R. 52 45N 39 35E
13 Lisboa, Portugal 38 42N 9 10W
9 Lisburn, N. Ireland 54 30N 6 2W
27 Lismore, Australia 28 44S 153 21E
9 Listowel, Ireland 52 27N 9 30W
37 Little Rock, U.S.A. 34 41N 92 10W
6 Liverpool, England 53 25N 3 0W
33 Livingstone, Zambia 17 50N 25 50E
14 Livorno, Italy 43 32N 10 18E
7 Lizard, Pt., England 49 57N 5 11W
14 Ljubljana, Yugoslavia 46 4N 14 33E
33 Lobito, Angola 12 18S 13 35E
40 Llanos, S. America 3 25N 71 35W
11 Lódz, Poland 51 45N 19 27E
16 Lofoten, Is., Norway 68 20N 14 0E
13 Logroño, Spain 42 28N 2 32W
12 Loire, R., France 47 25N 0 20W
23 Lombok, I., Indonesia 8 35S 116 20E
30 Lomé, Togo 6 9N 1 20E
35 London, Canada 43 0N 81 15W
7 London, England 51 30N 0 5W
9 Londonderry, N. Ireland 55 0N 7 20W
42 Londrina, Brazil 23 0S 51 10W
36 Long Beach, U.S.A. 33 46N 118 12W
37 Long I., U.S.A. 40 50N 73 20W
9 Longford, & Co., Ire. 53 43N 7 50W
13 Lorca, Spain 37 41N 1 42W
12 Lorient, France 47 45N 3 23W
36 Los Angeles, U.S.A. 34 0N 118 10W
8 Lothian, Co., Scotland 55 55N 3 15W
37 Louisville, U.S.A. 38 15N 85 45W
33 Lourenço Marques = Maputo, Mozambique 25 57S 32 34E
9 Louth, Co., Ireland 53 55N 6 30W
28 Lower Hutt, N.Z. 41 10S 174 55E
7 Lowestoft, England 52 29N 1 44E
25 Loyang, China 34 40N 112 28E
32 Lualaba, R., Zaïre 5 45S 26 50E
32 Luanda, Angola 8 58S 13 9E
33 Luanshya, Zambia 13 20S 28 8E
36 Lubbock, U.S.A. 33 40N 102 0W
11 Lublin, Poland 51 12N 22 38E
33 Lubumbashi, Zaïre 11 32S 27 28E
14 Lucca, Italy 43 50N 10 30E
25 Luchow, China 28 54N 105 17E
22 Lucknow, India 26 50N 81 0E
33 Lüderitz, S.W. Africa 26 37S 15 9E
22 Ludhiana, India 30 57N 75 56E
13 Lugo, Spain 43 2N 7 35W
16 Luleå, Sweden 65 35N 22 10E
33 Lusaka, Zambia 15 25S 28 15E
25 Lu-Ta, China 39 0N 121 31E
7 Luton, England 51 53N 0 24W
10 Luxembourg, st. Europe 50 0N 6 0E
10 Luzern, Switzerland 47 3N 8 18E
23 Luzon, I. Philippines 16 30N 121 30E
18 Lvov, U.S.S.R. 49 40N 24 0E
* 22 Lyallpur, Pakistan 31 30N 73 5E
16 Lycksele, Sweden 64 38N 18 40E
37 Lynchburg, U..SA. 37 23N 79 10W
12 Lyon, France 45 46N 4 50E
28 Lyttleton, N.Z. 43 35S 172 44E

M

25 Macau, China 22 16N 113 35E
41 Maceió, Brazil 9 40S 35 41W
9 Macgillycuddy's Reeks, Mts., Ireland 52 2N 9 45W
27 Mackay, Australia 21 36S 148 39E
34 Mackenzie, R., Can. 69 10N 134 20W
37 Macon, U.S.A. 32 50N 83 37W
9 Macroom, Ireland 51 54N 8 57W
33 Madagascar, st., Africa 19 0S 46 0E
30 Madeira, Is. Atlantic Oc. 32 50N 17 0W
40 Madeira, R., Brazil 5 30S 61 20W
37 Madison, U.S.A. 43 5N 89 25W
22 Madras, India 13 8N 80 19E
13 Madrid, Spain 40 25N 3 45W
22 Madurai, India 9 55N 78 10E
24 Maebashi, Japan 36 30N 139 0E
40 Magdalena, R., Colombia 8 30N 74 0W
10 Magdeburg, E. Germany 52 8N 11 36E
18 Magnitogorsk, U.S.S.R. 53 20N 59 0E

* Renamed Faisalabad

7 Maidstone, England 51 16N 0 31E
31 Maiduguri, Nigeria 12 0N 13 20E
10 Mainz, W. Germany 50 0N 8 17E
27 Maitland, Australia 32 44S 151 36E
23 Makasar, Str. of, Indon. 1 0S 118 20E
18 Makeyevka, U.S.S.R. 48 0N 38 0E
21 Makkah (Mecca), Saudi Arabia 21 30N 39 54E
23 Malacca, Str. of, Indonesia 3 0N 101 0E
13 Malaga, Spain 36 43N 4 23W
33 Malagasy Rep. st. = Madagascar 19 0S 46 0E
33 Malawi, L., Malawi 12 0S 34 30E
33 Malawi, st., Africa 13 0S 34 0E
23 Malaysia, Fed. of, Asia 5 23N 110 0E
22 Maldive Is., Indian Oc. 6 50N 73 0E
30 Mali, st., W. Africa 17 0N 4 0W
9 Malin Hd., Ireland 55 18N 7 16W
8 Mallaig, Scotland 57 0N 5 50W
13 Mallorca, I., Spain 39 30N 3 0E
9 Mallow, Ireland 52 8N 8 40W
17 Malmö, Sweden 55 33N 13 8E
14 Malta, st. Mediterranean Sea 35 50N 14 30E
6 Man, I. of, U.K. 54 15N 4 30W
23 Manado, Indonesia 1 40N 125 45E
39 Managua, Nicaragua 12 0N 86 20W
40 Manaus, Brazil 3 0S 60 0W
6 Manchester, England 53 30N 2 15W
37 Manchester, U.S.A. 42 58N 71 29W
22 Mandale, Burma 22 0N 96 10E
23 Manila, Philippines 14 40N 121 3E
34 Manitoba, L., Canada 50 40N 98 30W
40 Manizales, Colombia 5 10N 75 30W
10 Mannheim, W. Ger. 49 28N 8 29E
6 Mansfield, England 53 8N 1 12W
14 Mantova, (Mantua) Italy 45 10N 10 47E
28 Manukau, N.Z. 37 0S 174 56E
39 Manzanillo, Cuba 20 20N 77 10W
33 Maputo, Mozambique 25 57S 32 34E
42 Mar del Plata, Argentina 38 0S 57 30W
40 Maracaibo, Venezuela 10 37N 71 45W
40 Maracaibo, L. de, Ven. 9 40N 71 30W
40 Maracay, Venezuela 10 20N 67 35W
40 Margarita, I. de, Ven. 11 0N 64 0W
7 Margate, England 51 23N 1 24E
28 Maria van Diemen, C., N.Z. 34 29S 172 40E
3 Mariana Is., Pacific Oc. 17 0N 145 0E
39 Marianao, Cuba 23 8N 82 24W
14 Maribor, Yugoslavia 46 36N 15 40E
41 Marilia, Brazil 22 0S 50 0W
42 Maringá, Brazil 23 35S 51 50W
2 Marquesas Is., Pacific Oc. 9 30S 140 0W
30 Marrakech, Morocco 31 40N 8 0W
12 Marseille, France 43 18N 5 23E
3 Marshall Is., Pacific Oc. 9 0N 171 0E
39 Martinique, I., Fr. W. Indies 14 40N 61 0W
27 Maryborough, Austral. 25 31S 152 37E
39 Masaya, Nicaragua 12 0N 86 7W
21 Masqat, Oman 23 37N 58 36E
12 Massif Central, Mts., Fr. 45 30N 2 21E
28 Masterton, N.Z. 40 56S 175 39E
32 Matadi, Zaïre 5 52S 13 31E
39 Matagalpa, Nicaragua 13 10N 85 40W
38 Matamoros, Mexico 25 50N 97 30W
39 Matanzas, Cuba 23 0N 81 40W
24 Matsue, Japan 35 25N 133 10E
24 Matsuyama, Japan 33 45N 132 45E
30 Mauritania, st., Africa 20 0N 10 0W
29 Mauritius, st., Indian Oc. 20 0S 57 0E
39 Mayagüez, Puerto Rico 18 11N 67 8W
18 Maykop, U.S.S.R. 44 35N 40 25E
9 Mayo, Co., Ireland 53 47N 9 7W
38 Mazatlán, Mexico 23 10N 106 30W
32 Mbandaka, Zaïre 0 1S 18 18E
9 Meath, Co., Ireland 53 32N 6 40W
21 Mecca = Makkah
23 Medan, Indonesia 3 40N 98 38E
40 Medellín, Colombia 6 20N 75 45W
34 Medicine Hat, Canada 50 0N 110 45W
21 Medina = Al Madinah
4 Mediterranean Sea, Europe 35 0N 15 0E
22 Meerut, India 29 1N 77 50E
30 Meknés, Morocco 33 57N 5 39W
23 Mekong, R., Asia 18 0N 104 15E
27 Melbourne, Australia 37 40S 145 0E
30 Melilla Sp. Morocco 35 21N 2 57W
18 Melitopol, U.S.S.R. 46 50N 35 22E
26 Melville I., Australia 11 30S 131 0E
37 Memphis, U.S.A. 35 7N 90 0W
6 Menai, Str., Wales 53 7N 4 20W
42 Mendoza, Argentina 32 50S 68 52W
13 Menorca, I., Spain 40 0N 4 0E
42 Mercedes, Uruguay 33 12S 58 0W
23 Mergui Arch, Burma 11 30N 97 30E
38 Mérida, Mexico 20 50N 89 40W
6 Merseyside, Co., England 53 30N 3 0W
7 Merthyr Tydfil, Wales 51 45N 3 23W
14 Messina, & Str., Italy 38 10N 15 32E
33 Messina, S. Africa 22 20S 30 12E
12 Metz, France 49 8N 6 10E
38 Mexicali, Mexico 32 40N 115 30W
38 Mexico, st., America 20 0N 100 0N
38 Mexico, G. of, Central America 25 0N 90 0W
38 Mexico City, Mexico 19 20N 99 10W
37 Miami, U.S.A. 25 52N 80 15W
18 Miass, U.S.S.R. 54 59N 60 6E
37 Michigan, L., N. America 44 0N 87 0W
7 Mid Glamorgan, Co., Wales 51 35N 3 30W
33 Middelburg, S. Africa 31 30S 25 0E
6 Middlesbrough, England 54 34N 1 13W
36 Midland, U.S.A. 32 0N 102 3W
2 Midway I., Pacific Oc. 28 0N 178 0W
13 Mieres, Spain 43 18N 5 48W
14 Milano, (Milan) Italy 45 28N 9 10E
27 Mildura, Australia 34 8S 142 7E
7 Milford Haven, Wales 51 43N 5 2W
37 Milwaukee, U.S.A. 43 9N 87 58W
38 Minatitlán, Mexico 17 58N 94 35W
23 Mindanao, I., Philippines 8 0N 125 0E
37 Minneapolis, U.S.A. 44 58N 93 20W
18 Minsk, U.S.S.R. 53 52N 27 30E
11 Miskolc, Hungary 48 7N 20 50E
37 Mississippi, R., U.S.A. 41 0N 91 0W
36 Missouri, R., U.S.A. 38 40N 91 45W
9 Mizen Hd., Ireland 51 27N 9 50W
37 Mobile, U.S.A. 30 41N 88 3W
32 Mobutu Sese Seko, L., Africa 1 30N 31 0E
33 Moçambique, Mozam. 15 3S 40 42E
33 Moçambique, st. Africa 14 45S 38 30E
* 33 Moçâmedes, Angola 16 35S 12 30E
14 Módena, Italy 44 39N 10 55E
27 Moe, Australia 38 12S 146 19E
29 Mogadishu, Somalia 2 2N 45 25E
18 Mogilev, U.S.S.R. 53 55N 30 18E
17 Mölndal, Sweden 57 40N 12 3E
32 Mombasa, Kenya 4 0S 39 35E
12 Monaco, principality, Europe 43 36N 7 23E
9 Monaghan & Co., 54 15N 6 58W
38 Monclova, Mexico 26 50N 101 30W
35 Moncton, Canada 46 7N 64 51W
25 Mongolia, Rep., Asia 47 0N 103 0E
30 Monrovia, Liberia 6 18N 10 47W
12 Monte Carlo, Monaco 43 46N 7 23E
39 Montego Bay, Jamaica 18 30N 78 0W
38 Monterrey, Mexico 25 40N 100 30W
41 Montes Claros, Brazil 16 30S 43 50W
42 Montevideo, Uruguay 34 50S 56 11W
37 Montgomery, U.S.A. 32 20N 86 20W
12 Montluçon, France 46 22N 2 36E
12 Montpellier, France 43 37N 3 52E
35 Montreal, Canada 45 31N 73 34W
12 Montreuil, France 50 27N 1 45W
8 Montrose, Scotland 56 43N 2 28W
34 Moose Jaw, Canada 50 30N 105 30W
15 Morava, R., Cz. 49 50N 16 50E
8 Moray Firth, Scotland 57 50N 3 30W
6 Morecambe, England 54 5N 2 52W
38 Morelia, Mexico 19 40N 101 11W
30 Morocco, st., N. Africa 32 0N 5 0W
18 Moscow = Moskva
10 Mosel, R., Germany 49 48N 6 45E
16 Mosjøen, Norway 65 52N 13 20E
18 Moskva, U.S.S.R. 55 45N 37 35E
17 Moss, Norway 59 27N 10 40E
33 Mosselbaai, S. Africa 34 11S 22 8E
21 Mosul = Al Mawsil
17 Motala, Sweden 58 32N 15 1E
8 Motherwell, Scotland 55 48N 4 0W
27 Mount Gambier, Australia 37 38S 140 44E
27 Mount Isa, Australia 20 42S 139 26E
26 Mount Magnet, Australia 28 2S 117 47E
9 Mourne, Mts., N. Ire. 54 10N 6 0W
33 Mozambique Chan., Africa 20 0S 39 0E
33 Mozambique, Rep. Africa 23 30S 32 30E
32 Mtwara, Tanzania 10 20S 40 20E
33 Mufulira, Zambia 12 30S 28 0E
12 Mulhouse, France 47 44N 7 20E
8 Mull, I., Scotland 56 27N 6 0W
9 Mullinger, Ireland 53 31N 7 20W
22 Multan, Pakistan 30 15N 71 30E
10 Munchen, W. Germany 48 8N 11 33E
10 Münster, W. Germany 51 58N 7 37E
13 Murcia, Spain 38 2N 1 10W
18 Murmansk, U.S.S.R. 68 57N 33 10E
24 Muroran, Japan 42 25N 141 0E
27 Murray, R., Australia 35 50S 147 40E
21 Muscat = Masqat
32 Mweru, L., Zambia 9 0S 29 0E
22 Mysore, India 13 15N 77 0E

N

9 Naas, Ireland 53 12N 6 40W
24 Nagano, Japan 36 40N 138 10E
24 Nagasaki, Japan 32 47N 129 50E
24 Nagoya, Japan 35 10N 136 50E
22 Nagpur, India 21 8N 79 10E
32 Nairobi, Kenya 1 20S 36 50E
32 Nakuru, Kenya 0 15S 36 5E
16 Namsos, Norway 64 28N 11 35E
25 Nan Shan, China 38 0N 98 0E
34 Nanaimo, Canada 49 10N 124 0W
12 Nancy, France 48 42N 6 12E
25 Nanking, China 32 10N 118 50E
12 Nantes, France 47 12N 1 33W
28 Napier, N.Z. 39 30S 176 56E
14 Napoli (Naples) Italy 40 40N 14 5E
12 Narbonne, France 43 11N 3 0E
22 Narmada, R., India 22 40N 77 30E
27 Narrandera, Australia 34 42S 146 31E
26 Narrogin, Australia 32 58S 117 14E
16 Narvik, Norway 68 28N 17 35E
37 Nashville, U.S.A. 36 12N 86 46W
22 Nasik, India 20 2N 73 50E
39 Nassau, Bahamas 25 0N 77 30W
31 Nasser, L., Egypt 23 0N 32 30E
17 Nässjö, Sweden 57 38N 14 45E
41 Natal, Brazil 5 47S 35 13W
38 Navojoa, Mexico 27 0N 109 30W
15 Naxos, I., Greece 37 5N 25 30E
31 Ndjamena, Chad 12 4N 15 8E
33 Ndola, Zambia 13 0S 28 34E
9 Neagh, L., N. Ireland 54 35N 6 25W
42 Negro, R., Brazil 0 25S 64 0W
28 Nelson, N.Z. 41 18S 173 16E
9 Nenagh, Ireland 52 52N 8 11W
22 Nepal, St., Asia 28 0N 84 30E
8 Ness, L., Scotland 57 15N 4 30W
10 Netherlands, King. Europe 52 0N 5 30E
12 Nevers, France 47 0N 3 9E
37 New Bedford, U.S.A. 41 40N 70 52W
28 New Brighton, N.Z. 43 29S 172 43E
3 New Britain, I., Pacific Oc. 6 0S 151 0E
3 New Caledonia, I., Pacific Oc. 21 0S 165 0E
27 New England Ra., Australia 29 30S 152 0E
3 New Guinea, I., Australasia 4 0S 136 0E
37 New Haven, U.S.A. 41 20N 72 54W
** 3 New Hebrides Is., Pacific Oc. 15 0S 168 0E
3 New Ireland, I., Pacific Oc. 3 0S 151 30E
27 New Norfolk, Australia 44 46S 147 2E
37 New Orleans, U.S.A. 30 0N 90 0W

* Renamed Namibe
** Renamed Vanuatu

28 New Plymouth, N.Z. 39 4S 174 5E
39 New Providence, I., Bahamas 25 0N 77 30W
37 New York, U.S.A. 40 45N 74 0W
28 New Zealand, st., 40 0S 175 0E
37 Newark, U.S.A. 40 41N 74 12W
14 Newcastle, Australia 32 52S 151 49E
6 Newcastle, England 54 58N 1 37W
6 Newcastle-under-Lyme, England 53 2N 2 15W
7 Newfoundland, I., Can. 48 28N 56 0W
7 Newhaven, England, 50 47N 0 4E
7 Newmarket, England 52 15N 0 23E
7 Newport, Wales 52 1N 4 51W
37 Newport News , U.S.A. 37 0N 76 25W
9 Newtownards, N. Ire. 54 37N 5 40W
37 Niagara Falls, N. Amer. 43 5N 79 5W
30 Niamey, Niger 13 27N 2 6E
39 Nicaragua, st. Central America 11 40N 85 30W
14 Nice, France 43 42N 7 14E
22 Nicobar, Is., India 9 0N 93 0E
21 Nicosia = Levkôsia
30 Niger, st., Africa 15 30N 10 0E
30 Niger, R., Africa 13 35N 7 0E
30 Nigeria, st., W. Africa 8 30N 8 0E
24 Niigata, Japan 37 58N 139 0E
18 Nijmegen, Netherlands 51 50N 5 52E
18 Nikolayev, U.S.S.R. 46 58N 32 7E
30 Nile, R., Egypt 27 30N 30 30E
12 Nîmes, France 43 50N 4 23E
24 Ningpo, China 29 50N 121 30E
35 Nipigon, L., Canada 49 40N 88 30W
24 Nishinomiya, Japan 34 45N 135 20E
41 Niteroi, Brazil 22 52S 43 0W
18 Nizhniy Tagil, U.S.S.R. 57 45N 60 0E
38 Nogales, Mexico 31 36N 94 29W
34 Nome, Alaska 64 35N 165 40W
6 Norfolk, Co., England 52 39N 1 0E
37 Norfolk, U.S.A. 42 3N 97 25W
3 Norfolk I., Pacific Oc. 28 58S 168 3E
27 Normanton, Australia 17 40S 141 10E
17 Norrköping, Sweden 58 35N 16 10E
34 North Battleford, Canada 52 50N 108 10W
5 North Chan., British Isles 55 0N 5 30W
28 North I., N.Z. 38 0S 175 0E
25 North Korea, St., Asia 40 0N 127 0E
4 North Sea, Europe 55 0N 4 9E
8 North Uist, I., Scotland 57 40N 7 15W
6 North York Moors, England 54 25N 0 50W
6 North Yorkshire, Co., England 54 20N 1 30W
26 Northam, Australia 31 55S 116 42W
7 Northampton & Co., U.S.A 52 14N 0 54W
9 Northern Ireland, United Kingdom 54 45N 7 0W
6 Northumberland, Co., England 55 12N 2 0W
16 Norway, King. Europe 67 0N 11 0E
6 Norwich, England 52 38N 1 17E
6 Nottingham & Co., 52 57N 1 10W
3 Nouméa, New Caledonia 22 17S 166 30E
33 Nova Lisboa, see Huambo, Angola 12 42S 15 54W
14 Novara, Italy 45 27N 8 36E
18 Novaya Zemlya, Is., U.S.S.R. 75 0N 56 0E
18 Novgorod, U.S.S.R. 58 30N 31 25E
15 Novi Sad, Yugoslavia 45 18N 19 52E
18 Novokuznetsk, U.S.S.R. 52 50S 87 50E
18 Novomoskovsk, U.S.S.R. 54 5N 38 15E
18 Novorossiysk, U.S.S.R. 44 43N 37 52E
18 Novosibirsk, U.S.S.R. 55 0N 83 5E
38 Nueva Rosita, Mexico 28 0N 101 20W
7 Nuneaton, England 53 32 1 29W
18 Nürnberg, W. Germany 49 26N 11 5E
33 Nyasa, L., Africa 12 0S 34 30E

O

36 Oahu, I., Hawaiian Is. 21 30N 158 0W
37 Oak Ridge, U.S.A. 36 1N 84 5W
36 Oakland, U.S.A. 37 50N 122 18W
28 Oamaru, N.Z. 45 5S 170 59E
38 Oaxaca, Mexico 17 2N 96 40W
18 Ob, R., U.S.S.R. 62 40N 66 0E
8 Oban, Scotland 56 25N 5 30W
40 Occidental, Cordillera, Colombia 5 0N 76 0W
16 Odense, Denmark 55 26N 10 26E
18 Odessa, U.S.S.R. 41 30S 30 45E
18 Odra, R. Poland 52 40N 14 28E
9 Offaly, Co., Ireland 53 15N 7 30W
30 Ogbomosho, Nigeria 8 1N 3 29E
36 Ogden, U.S.A. 41 13N 112 1W
37 Ohio, R., U.S.A. 39 40N 80 50W
24 Óita, Japan 33 15N 131 36E
33 Okavango Swamps, Botswana 19 30S 23 0E
24 Okayama, Japan 34 40N 133 44E
24 Okazaki, Japan 34 36N 137 0E
19 Okhotsk, Sea of, Asia 55 0N 145 0E
37 Oklahoma City, U.S.A. 35 25N 97 30W
37 Oklahoma, st., U.S.A. 35 20N 97 30W
17 Öland, I., Sweden 56 45N 16 50E
18 Oldenburg, W. Germany 53 10N 8 10E
6 Oldham, England 53 33N 2 8W
15 Ólimbos, Oros, (Olympus) Greece 40 6N 22 23E
15 Olympia, Greece 37 39N 21 39E
21 Oman, G. of, S.W. Asia 24 30N 58 30E
21 Oman, Sultanate, Asia 20 0N 58 0E
9 Omagh, N. Ireland 54 36N 7 20W
37 Omaha, U.S.A. 41 15N 96 0W
30 Omdurmân, Sudan 15 40N 32 28E
24 Omiya, Japan 36 0N 139 32E
18 Omsk, U.S.S.R. 55 0N 73 38E
28 Onehunga, N.Z. 36 55S 174 30E
30 Onitsha, Nigeria 6 6N 6 42E
37 Ontario, L., N. America 43 40N 78 0W
11 Oradea, Rumania 47 2N 21 58E
30 Oran, Algeria 36 45N 0 39W

33 Orange, R., S. Africa 29 50S 24 45E
33 Orange, R., S. Africa 28 30S 18 0E
18 Ordzhonikidze, U.S.S.R. 43 0N 44 30E
17 Orebro, Sweden 59 20N 15 18E
18 Orel, U.S.S.R. 52 57N 36 3E
18 Orenburg, U.S.S.R. 52 0N 55 5E
12 Orense, Spain 42 19N 7 55W
12 Orléans, France 47 54N 1 52E
40 Orinoco, R., Venezuela 8 0N 65 30W
38 Orizaba, Mexico 18 50N 97 10W
8 Orkney, Is., Scotland 59 0N 3 0W
37 Orlando, U.S.A. 28 30N 81 25W
17 Örnsköldsvik, Sweden 63 17N 18 50E
18 Orsha, U.S.S.R. 54 30N 30 25E
18 Orsk, U.S.S.R. 51 20N 58 34E
40 Oruro, Bolivia 18 0S 67 19W
24 Osaka, Japan 34 40N 135 30E
30 Oshogbo, Nigeria 7 48N 4 37E
15 Osijek, Yugoslavia 43 34N 18 41E
17 Oskarshamn, Sweden 57 15N 16 25E
16 Oslo, Norway 59 53N 10 52E
16 Östersund, Sweden 63 10N 14 45E
11 Ostrava, Czechoslovakia 49 51N 18 18E
15 Otranto, Str. of, Adriatic Sea 40 15N 19 0E
35 Ottawa, Canada 45 27N 75 42W
30 Ouagadougou, B. Faso 12 25N 1 30W
30 Oubangi, R., Zaïre 1 0N 17 50E
30 Oujda, Morocco 34 45N 2 0W
16 Oulu, Finland 64 25N 27 30E
7 Ouse, R., England 52 12N 0 7E
8 Outer Hebrides, Is., Scotland
13 Oviedo, Spain 43 25N 5 50W
7 Oxford & Co., 51 45N 1 15W
30 Oyo, Nigeria 7 46N 3 56E

P

38 Pachuca, Mexico 20 10N 98 40W
2 Pacific Ocean 10 0N 140 0W
23 Padang, Indonesia 1 0S 100 20E
14 Pádova, Italy 45 24N 11 52E
8 Paisley, Scotland 55 51N 4 27W
22 Pakistan, St., Asia 30 0N 70 0E
23 Palawan, I., Philippines 10 0N 119 0E
23 Palembang, Indonesia 3 0S 104 50E
13 Palencia, Spain 42 1N 4 34W
14 Palermo, Italy 38 8N 13 20E
13 Palma, Spain 39 33N 2 39E
28 Palmerston North, N.Z. 40 21S 175 39E
40 Palmira, Colombia 3 32N 76 16W
13 Pamplona, Spain 42 48N 1 38W
38 Panama, Panama 9 0N 79 25W
39 Panama, Rep., Central America 9 0N 79 35W
23 Panay, I., Philippines 11 0N 122 30E
14 Pantelleria, I., Italy 36 52N 12 0E
25 Paotow, China 40 45 110 0E
3 Papua New Guinea, st., Australasia 8 0S 145 0E
42 Paraguay, R., Paraguay 24 30S 58 20W
42 Paraguay, Rep., S. Amer. 23 0S 57 0W
41 Paramaribo, Surinam 5 50N 55 10W
42 Paraná, Argentina 32 0S 60 30W
42 Paraná, R., Argentine 33 43S 59 15W
12 Paris, France 48 50N 2 20E
27 Parkes, Australia 33 9S 148 11E
14 Parma, Italy 44 50N 10 20E
35 Parry Sound, Canada 45 20N 80 0W
36 Pasadena, U.S.A. 34 5N 118 0W
22 Patna, India 23 35N 85 18E
15 Patrai, Greece 38 14N 21 47E
12 Pau, France 43 19N 0 25W
14 Pavia, Italy 45 10N 9 10E
18 Pavlodar, U.S.S.R. 52 33N 77 0E
15 Pazardzhik, Bulgaria 42 12N 24 20E
11 Pécs, Hungary 46 5N 18 15E
24 Peiping, China 39 50N 116 20E
23 Pekalongan, Indonesia 6 53S 109 40E
42 Pelotas, Brazil 31 42S 52 23W
7 Pembroke, Wales 51 40N 5 0W
23 Penang, I., Malaysia 5 25N 100 15E
25 Pengpu, China 33 0N 117 25E
24 Penki, China 41 20N 123 50E
6 Pennines, Rd., England 54 50N 2 20W
34 Penticton, Canada 49 30N 119 30W
8 Pentland Firth, 58 43N 3 10W
18 Penza, U.S.S.R. 53 15N 45 5E
7 Ponzanee, England 50 7N 5 32W
37 Peoria, U.S.A. 40 40N 89 40W
40 Pereira, Colombia 4 50N 75 40W
18 Perm, U.S.S.R. 58 0N 56 10E
12 Perpignan, France 42 42N 2 53E
* 21 Persian G., Asia 27 0N 50 0E
26 Perth, Australia 31 57S 115 52E
8 Perth, Scotland 56 24N 3 27W
40 Peru, Rep., S. America 8 0S 75 0W
14 Perúgia, Italy 43 6N 12 24E
18 Pervouralsk, U.S.S.R. 56 55N 60 0E
14 Pésaro, Italy 43 55N 12 53E
41 Pescara, Italy 42 28N 14 13E
22 Peshawar, Pakistan 34 2N 71 37E
33 Peterboro', Canada 44 20N 78 20W
27 Peterborough, Australia 33 0S 138 45E
7 Peterborough, England 52 35N 0 14W
8 Peterhead, Scotland 57 30N 1 49W
28 Petone, N.Z. 41 13S 174 53E
33 Petermaritzburg, S. Africa 29 35S 29 25E
19 Petropavlovsk, U.S.S.R. 55 0N 69 0E
19 Petropavlovsk-Kamchatskiy, U.S.S.R. 53 16N 159 0E
18 Petrozavosdk, U.S.S.R. 61 41N 34 20E
23 Phan Bho Ho Chi Minh, Vietnam 10 58N 106 40E
37 Philadelphia, U.S.A. 40 0N 75 10W
23 Philippines, Rep., Asia 12 0N 123 0E
23 Phnom Penh, Cambodia 11 33N 104 55E
36 Phoenix, U.S.A. 33 30N 112 10W
2 Phoenix Is., Pacific Oc. 3 30S 172 0W
14 Piacenza, Italy 45 3N 9 41E
28 Picton, N.Z. 41 18S 174 3E
38 Piedras Negras, Mexico 28 35N 100 35W
33 Pietermaritzburg, S. Africa 23 54S 29 25E
33 Pietersburg, S. Africa 23 54S 29 25E

*   *Also known as The Gulf*

39 Pinar del Rio, Cuba 22 26N 83 40W
12 Pindos Oros, Greece 40 0N 21 0E
41 Piracicaba, Brazil 22 45S 47 30W
15 Piraeus = Piraiévs
15 Piraiévs, Greece 37 57N 23 42E
14 Pisa, Italy 43 43N 10 23E
2 Pistóia, Italy 43 19N 10 53E
2 Pitcairn I., Pacific Oc. 25 5S 130 5W
16 Piteå, Sweden 65 55N 21 25E
8 Pitlochry, Scotland 56 43N 3 43W
37 Pittsburgh, U.S.A. 40 25N 79 55W
40 Piura, Peru 5 5S 80 45W
42 Plata, Rio de la, S. America 35 30S 56 0W
37 Platte, R., U.S.A. 41 0N 98 0W
18 Plauen, W. Germany 50 29N 12 9E
8 Plenty, B. of, N.Z. 37 45S 177 0E
15 Pleven, Bulgaria 43 26N 24 37E
15 Plovdir, Bulgaria 42 8N 24 44E
7 Plymouth, England 50 23N 4 9W
11 Plzen, Czechoslovakia 49 5N 13 22E
19 Po, R., Italy 45 0N 10 45E
39 Pointe-à-Pitre, Guadaloupe 16 10N 61 30W
12 Pointe-Noire, Congo 4 48S 12 0E
12 Poitiers, France 46 35N 0 20W
11 Poland, st., Europe 52 0N 20 0E
18 Poltava, U.S.S.R. 49 35N 34 35E
39 Ponce, Puerto Rico 18 0N 66 50W
42 Ponta Grossa, Brazil 25 0S 50 10W
42 Pontevedra, Spain 42 26N 8 40W
23 Pontianak, Indonesia 0 3S 109 15E
7 Poole, England 50 42N 2 2W
22 Poona, India 18 29N 73 57E
21 Pori, Finland 61 27N 21 50E
39 Port-au-Prince, Haiti 18 40N 72 20W
28 Port Augusta, Australia 32 30S 137 50E
33 Port Elizabeth, S. Africa 33 58S 25 40E
8 Port Glasgow, Scotland 55 57N 4 40W
30 Port Harcourt, Nigeria 4 40N 7 10E
26 Port Hedland, Australia 20 25S 118 35E
9 Port Laoise, Ireland 53 2N 7 20W
26 Port Lincoln, Australia 34 42S 135 52E
27 Port Macquarie, Australia 31 25S 152 54E
3 Port Moresby, Papua New Guinea 9 24S 147 8E
39 Port of Spain, Trinidad 10 40N 61 20W
27 Port Pirie, Australia 33 10S 137 58E
31 Port Said = Bûr Saîd 31 28N 32 6E
31 Port Sudan = Bûr Sûdân 31 28N 32 6E
7 Port Talbot, Wales 51 35N 3 48W
34 Portage la Prairie, Canada 49 58N 98 18W
36 Portland, U.S.A. 45 35N 122 40W
7 Portland Bill, Pt., England 50 31N 2 27W
13 Pôrto, Portugal 41 8N 8 40W
42 Pôrto Alegre, Brazil 30 5S 51 3W
7 Portree, Scotland 57 25N 6 11W
7 Portsmouth, England 50 48N 1 6W
37 Portsmouth, U.S.A. 36 50N 76 20W
13 Portugal, Rep., Europe 40 0N 7 0W
42 Posadas, Spain 37 47N 5 11W
40 Potosi, Bolivia 19 38S 65 50W
18 Potsdam, Germany 52 23N 13 4E
7 Powys, Co., Wales 52 30N 3 30W
11 Poznan, Poland 52 25N 17 0E
11 Praha (Prague) Cz. 50 5N 14 22E
14 Prato, Italy 43 53N 11 5E
6 Preston, England 53 46N 2 42W
8 Prestwick, Scotland 55 30N 4 38W
33 Pretoria, S. Africa 25 44S 28 12E
34 Prince Albert, Canada 53 15N 105 50W
35 Prince Edward I., Canada 46 20N 63 0W
34 Prince George, Canada 53 50N 122 50W
34 Prince Rupert, Canada 54 20N 130 20W
18 Prokopyevsk, 54 0N 87 3E
16 Prome, Burma 18 45N 95 30E
37 Providence, U.S.A. 41 41N 71 15W
34 Prudhoe Bay, Australia 21 30S 149 30W
18 Pskov, U.S.S.R. 57 50N 28 25E
36 Pueblo, Mexico 19 0N 98 10W
36 Pueblo, U.S.A. 38 20N 104 40W
42 Puerto Montt, Chile 41 22S 72 40W
39 Puerto Plata, Dominican Rep. 19 40N 70 45W
39 Puerto Rico, I., W. Indies 18 10N 66 30W
14 Pula, Yugoslavia 44 54N 13 57E
22 Punakha, Bhutan 27 42N 89 52E
42 Punta Arenas, Chile 53 0S 71 0W
39 Puntarenas, Costa Rica 10 0N 84 50W
40 Purus, R., Brazil 5 25S 64 0W
24 Pusan, S. Korea 35 5N 129 0E
25 Pyongyang, N. Korea 39 0N 125 30E
13 Pyrénées, Mts., Europe 42 45N 1 0E

Q

21 Qatar, st., Asia 25 30N 51 15E
31 Qena, Egypt 26 10N 32 43E
35 Quebec, Canada 46 52N 71 13W
34 Queen Charlotte Is., Canada 53 10N 132 0W
2 Queen Elizabeth Is., Canada 75 0N 95 0W
33 Quelimane, Mozambique 17 53S 36 58E
38 Querétaro, Mexico 20 40N 100 23W
22 Quetta, Pakistan 30 15N 66 55E
23 Quezon City, Phil. 14 50N 121 0E
40 Quimper, France 48 0N 4 9W
40 Quito, Ecuador 0 15S 78 35W

R

30 Rabat, Morocco 33 9N 6 53W
3 Rabaul, Papua New Guinea 4 24S 152 18E
14 Ragusa, Italy 36 56N 14 42E
22 Rajkot, India 22 15N 70 56E

37 Raleigh, U.S.A. 35 46N 78 38W
17 Randers, Denmark 56 29N 10 1E
16 Rangoon, Burma 16 45N 96 20E
28 Rarotonga, I., Pacific Oc. 21 30S 160 0W
21 Rasht, Iran 37 20N 49 40E
9 Rathlin, I., N. Ireland 55 18N 6 14W
17 Rauma, Finland 61 10N 21 30E
14 Ravenna, Italy 44 28N 12 15E
22 Rawalpindi, Pakistan 33 38N 73 8E
7 Reading, England 51 27N 0 57W
41 Recife, Brazil 8 0S 35 0W
34 Red Dear, Canada 52 20N 113 50W
21 Red Sea, Africa/Asia 25 0N 36 0E
18 Regensburg, W. Germany 49 1N 12 7E
14 Réggio, Italy 38 7N 15 38E
34 Regina, Canada 50 30N 104 35W
12 Reims, France 49 15N 4 0E
16 Reindeer L., Canada 57 22N 102 20W
12 Rennes, France 48 7N 1 41W
36 Reno, U.S.A. 39 30N 119 50W
42 Resistencia, Argentina 27 30N 59 0W
16 Réunion, I., Indian Oc. 22 0S 56 0E
16 Revelstoke, Canada 51 0N 118 0W
16 Reykjavik, Iceland 64 10N 22 0W
15 Rhodes = Ródhos, I.
* 33 Rhodesia, st., Africa 19 0S 29 0E
12 Rhine, R., W. Germany 51 42N 6 20E
41 Rhondda, Wales 51 40N 3 30W
12 Rhône, R., France 43 28N 4 42E
21 Rhum, I., Scotland 57 0N 6 20W
41 Ribeirvo Prêto, Brazil 21 10S 47 50W
32 Riccarton, N.Z. 43 32S 172 37E
36 Richland, U.S.A. 46 15N 119 15W
37 Richmond, U.S.A. 37 33N 77 27W
16 Riga, U.S.S.R. 56 58N 24 12E
15 Rijeka, Yugoslavia 45 20N 14 21E
14 Rímini, Italy 44 3N 12 33E
35 Rimouski, Canada 48 27N 68 30W
41 Rio de Janeiro, Brazil 22 50S 43 0W
30 Rio Gallegos, Arg. 51 45S 69 20W
26 Rio Grande, Brazil 32 0S 52 20W
38 Rio Grande, R., U.S.A. 35 45N 106 20W
35 Rivière du Loup, Canada 47 50N 69 30W
21 Riyadh, see Ar Riyal 24 40N 46 50E
36 Roanoke, U.S.A. 37 19N 79 55W
6 Rochdale, England 53 36N 2 10W
12 Rochefort, France 45 56N 0 57W
37 Rochester, U.S.A. 43 10N 77 40W
37 Rockford, U.S.A. 42 20N 89 0W
27 Rockhampton, Australia 23 22S 150 32E
36 Rocky Mts., N. America 48 0N 113 0W
15 Ródhos, I., Greece 36 15N 28 10E
27 Roma, Australia 26 32S 148 49E
14 Roma, (Rome) Italy 41 54N 12 30E
42 Rosario, Argentina 33 0S 60 50W
9 Roscommon & Co., Ireland 53 38N 8 11W
16 Roskilde, Denmark 55 38N 12 3E
2 Ross Dependency, Antarctica 70 0S 170 5W
3 Ross Sea, Antarctica 74 0S 178 0E
18 Rostock, E. Germany 54 4N 12 9E
18 Rostov, U.S.S.R., 47 15N 39 45E
8 Rosyth, Scotland 56 2N 3 26W
6 Rotherham, England 53 26N 1 21W
18 Rothesay, Scotland 55 50N 5 3W
28 Rotorua, N.Z. 38 9S 176 16E
18 Rotterdam, Neth. 51 55N 4 30E
12 Roubaix, France 50 40N 3 10E
12 Rouen, France 49 27N 1 4E
35 Rouyn, Canada 48 20N 79 0W
16 Rovaniemi, Finland 66 29N 25 41E
18 Rovno, U.S.S.R. 50 40N 26 10E
21 Rub'al Khali, desert, Saudi Arabia 21 0N 51 0E
7 Rugby, England 52 23N 1 16W
** 11 Rumania, st. Europe 46 0N 25 0E
18 Ruse, Bulgaria 43 48N 25 59E
8 Rutherglen, Scotland 55 50N 4 11W
32 Rwanda, st., Africa 2 30S 30 0E
18 Ryazan, U.S.S.R. 54 40N 39 40E
† 18 Rybinsk, U.S.S.R. 58 5N 38 50E

S

10 Saarbrücken, W. Germany 49 15N 6 58E
13 Sabadell, Spain 41 28N 2 7E
23 Sabah, Malaysia 6 0N 117 0E
34 Sable, C., Canada 43 29N 65 38W
37 Sacremento, U.S.A. 38 39N 121 30E
37 Saginaw, U.S.A. 43 26N 83 55W
30 Sahara, desert, Africa 23 0N 5 0W
23 Saigon, see Phan Bho Ho Chi Minh, Vietnam 10 58N 106 40E
7 St. Albans, England 51 44N 0 19W
34 St. Andrews, Scotland 56 20N 2 48W
7 St. Austell, England 50 20N 4 48W
34 St. Boniface, Canada 49 50N 97 10W
39 St. Christopher, I., W. Indies 17 20N 62 40W
7 St. David's Hd., Wales 51 54N 5 16W
12 St. Etienne, France 45 27N 4 22E
5 St. George's Chan., Br. Isles 52 0N 6 0W
6 St. Helena, I., Atlantic Oc. 15 55S 5 44W
6 St. Helens, England 53 28N 2 43W
35 St. Hyacinthe, Canada 45 40N 72 58W
34 Saint John, Canada 45 20N 66 8W
35 St. John's, Canada 47 33N 52 40W
37 St. Joseph, U.S.A. 39 46N 94 50W
28 St. Kilda, N.Z. 45 53S 170 31E
35 St. Lawrence, G. of, Canada 48 25N 62 0W
35 St. Lawrence, St., Canada 49 30N 66 0W
30 St. Louis, Senegal 16 8N 16 27W
37 St. Louis, U.S.A. 38 40N 90 20W
39 St. Lucia, I., Windward Is., 14 0N 60 50W
12 St. Malo, France 48 40 2 0W

*   *Renamed Zimbabwe*
** *Also known as Romania*
†   *Renamed Andropov*

12 St. Nazaire, France 47 18N 2 11W
34 St. Paul, U.S.A. 44 54N 93 5W
37 St. Petersburg, U.S.A. 27 45N 82 40W
35 St. Pierre et Miquelon, N. America 46 49N 56 15W
12 St. Quentin, France 49 55N 3 20E
39 St. Vincent, I., Windward Is., 13 10N 61 10W
24 Sakai, Japan 34 35N 135 27E
19 Sakhalin, I., U.S.S.R. 51 0N 143 0E
35 Salado, R., 25 40S 58 10W
13 Salamanca, Spain 40 57N 5 40W
18 Salem, India 11 39N 78 12E
14 Salerno, Italy 40 40N 14 44E
7 Salisbury, England 51 4N 1 48W
* 33 Salisbury, Zimbabwe 17 50N 31 2E
7 Salisbury Plain, England 51 13N 2 0W
41 Salvador, Brazil 13 0S 38 30W
38 Salvador, st., Central America 13 50N 89 0W
36 Salt Lake City, U.S.A. 40 45N 112 0W
42 Salta, Argentina 24 48S 65 30W
38 Saltillo, Mexico 25 30N 100 57W
10 Salzburg, Austria 47 48N 13 2E
23 Samar, I., Philippines 12 0N 125 0E
18 Samarkand, U.S.S.R. 39 40N 67 0E
36 Samsun, Turkey 41 15N 36 15E
36 San Angelo, U.S.A. 31 30N 100 30W
36 San Antonio, U.S.A. 29 30N 98 30W
40 San Cristóbal, Ven. 7 35N 72 24W
36 San Diego, U.S.A. 32 50N 117 10W
39 San Fernando, Trinidad 37 45N 122 30W
36 San Francisco, U.S.A. 37 45N 122 30W
39 San Francisco de Macoris, Dominican Rep. 19 19N 70 15W
36 San Jose, Costa Rica 10 0N 84 2W
36 San Jose, U.S.A. 37 10N 121 57W
39 San Juan, Puerto Rico 18 29N 66 6W
38 San Luis Potosí, Mex. 22 10N 101 0W
14 San Marino, Rep. Italy 43 56N 12 5E
42 San Miguel de Tucumán, Argentina 26 47S 65 13W
38 San Pedro de las Colonias, Mexico 25 50N 102 59W
38 San Salvador, Salvador 13 40N 89 20W
13 San Sebastian, Spain 43 17N 1 58W
21 San'a, Yemen 15 27N 44 12E
17 Sancti Spiritus, Cuba 21 52N 79 33W
17 Sandviken, Sweden 60 38N 16 46E
36 Santa Ana, Salvador 14 0N 89 40W
36 Santa Ana, U.S.A. 33 48N 117 55W
36 Santa Barbara, U.S.A. 34 25N 119 40W
36 Santa Barbara Is., U.S.A. 33 40N 119 40W
39 Santa Clara, Cuba 22 20N 80 0W
42 Santa Cruz, Tenerife 28 29N 16 26W
42 Santa Fé, Argentina 31 35S 60 41W
40 Santa Marta, Colombia 11 15N 74 13W
13 Santander, Spain 43 27N 3 51W
41 Santarém, Brazil 2 25S 54 42W
42 Santiago, Chile 33 24S 70 50W
39 Santiago, Dominican Rep. 19 30N 70 40W
13 Santiago, Spain 42 52N 8 37W
39 Santiago de Cuba, Cuba 20 0N 75 49W
42 Santiago del Estero, Argentina 27 50S 64 20W
39 Santo Domingo, Dominican Rep. 18 30N 69 58W
42 Santos, Brazil 24 0S 46 20W
42 São Carlos, Brazil 22 0S 47 50W
41 São Luis, Brazil 2 39S 44 15W
42 São Marcos, B. de, Brazil 2 0S 44 0W
42 Sao Paulo, Brazil 23 40S 46 50W
12 São Roque, C. de, Brazil 5 30S 35 10W
12 Saône, R., France 46 25N 4 50E
24 Sapporo, Japan 43 0N 141 15E
15 Sarajevo, Yugoslavia 43 52N 18 26E
18 Saransk, U.S.S.R. 54 10N 45 10E
18 Saratov, U.S.S.R. 51 30N 46 2E
23 Sarawak, Malaysia 2 0N 113 0E
14 Sardinia, I., Italy 40 0N 9 0E
17 Sarpsborg, Norway 59 16N 11 12E
24 Sasebo, Japan 33 15N 129 50E
34 Saskatoon, Canada 52 10N 106 45W
14 Sássari, Italy 40 44N 8 33E
21 Saudi Arabia, st., Asia 26 0N 44 0E
35 Saulte Ste. Marie, Canada 46 30N 84 20W
15 Sava, R., Yugoslavia 44 40N 19 50E
37 Savannah, U.S.A. 32 4N 81 4W
17 Savona, Italy 44 19N 8 29E
6 Sca Fell, Pk., England 54 27N 3 14W
7 Scarborough, England 54 17N 0 24W
7 Scilly, Is., England 49 55N 6 15W
8 Scotland, U.K. 57 0N 4 0W
37 Scranton, U.S.A. 41 22N 75 41W
6 Scunthorpe, England 53 35N 0 38W
36 Seattle, U.S.A. 47 36N 122 20W
12 Seine, R., France 49 28N 0 15E
18 Semipalatinsk, U.S.S.R. 50 30N 80 10E
24 Sendai, Japan 38 15N 140 53E
30 Senegal, R., Senegal 16 30N 15 30W
30 Senegal, st., W. Africa 14 30N 14 30W
35 Sept Îles, Canada 50 13 66 22W
18 Serov, U.S.S.R. 59 40N 60 20E
33 Serowe, Botswana 22 18S 26 58E
12 Sète, France 43 25N 3 42E
13 Setúbal, Portugal 38 30N 8 58W
18 Sevastopol, U.S.S.R. 44 35N 33 30E
7 Severn, R., U.K. 52 15N 2 13W
18 Severodvinsk, U.S.S.R. 64 27N 39 58E
13 Sevilla, Spain 37 25N 6 0W
34 Seward, Alaska 60 0N 149 30W
20 Seychelles, Is., Indian Oc. 5 0S 56 0E
31 Sfax, Tunisia 34 49N 10 40E
18 Shakhty, U.S.S.R. 47 0N 40 10E
25 Shanghai, China 31 15N 121 30E
37 Shantow, China 23 25N 116 40E
9 Shannon, R., Ireland 53 10N 8 10W
6 Sheffield, England 53 23N 1 28W
27 Shellharbour, Australia 34 31S 150 51E

*   *Renamed Harare*